S0-DVE-556

Burton L. Schweitzer
Manchester Community College

Howell Aarons
Mohegan Community College

WORD ATTACK
An Individualized Approach

Charles E. Merrill Publishing Company
A Bell & Howell Company
Columbus   Toronto   London   Sydney

Published by
Charles E. Merrill Publishing Co.
A Bell & Howell Company
Columbus, Ohio 43216

This book was set in Baskerville and Optima.
Cover Design Coordination: Will Chenoweth
Production Coordination: Linda Hillis Bayma

Copyright © 1980 by Bell & Howell Company. All rights reserved. No part of this book may be reproduced in any form, electronic or mechanical, including photocopy, recording, or any information storage and retrieval system, without permission in writing from the publisher.

International Standard Book Number: 0–675–08187–4

2 3 4 5 6 7 8 9 10—85 84 83 82 81

Printed in the United States of America

Preface

Successful word recognition is fundamental to reading. It is the base upon which successful reading is built. This audiotutorial program is designed to help students improve their word attack skills.

When students are confronted with a new word which frustrates their attempts to grasp the meaning of a passage, they may react in a variety of ways. First, they may ask someone for help with the word. Second, they may get clues from accompanying illustrations. Third, they may get the meaning through other words in the sentence.

Certainly all of these methods for learning to recognize words are useful. However, students are often limited to just these methods. In our work with reading students at all levels, we have found that students may have the ability to comprehend material, but that material may be inaccessible because it contains many unknown words. When one word is unfamiliar and cannot be pronounced, the meaning of a whole phrase may be lost. Without the phrase, the sentence is lost, without the sentence, the paragraph is lost; without the paragraph, the selection is lost. Other skills, then, are necessary for recognizing unfamiliar words in more limited contexts to avoid such an expanding chain of confusion. These skills are often referred to as "word attack skills."

The program: *Word Attack: An Individualized Approach* reviews, presents, explains, and gives practice in both the *oral* and *written* word attack skills needed to pronounce and read unknown words. Its goal is to enable students to develop independence in reading effectively. In keeping with this objective, the program has been designed exclusively for an individualized and self-pacing approach. The program is unique in that it introduces, teaches, reviews, and reinforces word attack skills through combined auditory, visual, and kinesthetic methods of instruction.

The authors wish to thank their editor at Merrill, Gil Imholz, for his invaluable assistance in helping them to organize the material in its final format. Thanks are also extended to Dr. Jack Bagford, Professor of Education at the University of Iowa, and to Ms. June Dempsey, Chairperson, Developmental Education, San Joaquin Delta College, for their ideas and suggestions regarding the format, teaching methods, and exercises in the program.

There would be no program without the patience, understanding, and suggestions made by our families. For their parts, then, in helping to make this program a reality, we wish to offer special thanks to our wives, June Schweitzer and Trudy Aarons, and to our children–Matthew, Robert, Gregg, and Leslie Schweitzer and Beth, Wendy, Ellen, and Marci Aarons.

To the Students

Word Attack: An Individualized Approach is designed to help you develop the ability to pronounce unfamiliar words. It does this in a step-by-step manner by taking you from the most basic concepts of consonants through the more complicated skills of syllabication and dictionary use.

The program's approach is unique because it allows you to *see and hear* the relationships between sounds and their symbols. Many times you will be asked to write answers in the worktext in response to the skilltape. As you do this, your ability to sound out words will improve.

The use of the tape recorder in *Word Attack: An Individualized Approach* allows you ·to work at your own pace. You can go back as often as necessary to help you understand concepts. In addition to instruction, the skilltape often gives answers to exercises, so you know immediately whether you are right or wrong.

Learning word attack skills is like building a house. The first chapter of the worktext and skilltape creates the foundation for this learning. Each chapter builds on the previous chapter. One chapter, in itself, is not enough to teach you to sound out all new words to complete the task. By the time you finish the program, however, you will build up enough knowledge to pronounce many unfamiliar words.

Before starting the program your instructor will give you some basic directions on how to use the worktext and the skilltapes. Although this program is individualized and allows you to work at your own pace, you should consult with your instructor at the end of each chapter and whenever you have any difficulties while working through the program.

Here are some simple instructions for using this program:

1. Each chapter begins with a glossary of the technical vocabulary used in that section. You should become familiar with these words.

2. Read the introduction to each chapter. The introduction describes the kinds of skills that will be presented and what you will know when you complete the chapter.

3. Following the introduction are the pretests. Take the pretests before working through the chapter. After taking the test you should check your answers with those at the end of the chapter. If you score 90 percent, or better, take the posttests near the end of the chapter. If you score less than 90 percent on the pretests or posttest, you should work through the entire chapter. The score which equals 90 percent correct is indicated following each pretest and posttest section.

4. If you are working through this program by yourself, with or without the supervision of an instructor, you should do the following:

   (a) Carefully follow all directions on the skilltape and in the worktext. Be particularly careful to follow directions telling you to turn on and turn off the skilltape. Each new section of the skilltape begins with an announcement, such as "This portion of the skilltape begins Exercise . . . . " Since you are working on your own, you are the one who controls the speed of working through the material. When you are listening to a skilltape, you may repeat or play back the skilltape as many times as necessary in order to hear the directions, listen to explanations of the answers, or listen to the skill exercises.

   (b) After you complete each exercise, you should make your corrections immediately and then record your scores (number correct) in the spaces provided following the exercise and on the summary sheet at the end of each chapter.

5. If you are working with an instructor, you should show him or her the summary sheet and the work in your worktext when you have completed all the exercises in a chapter as well as the posttests. The instructor will determine whether you should be directed to additional exercises for certain skills and whether further posttests are necessary.

6. If you are working through this program under the direction of a tutor, paraprofessional, or instructor, he or she may also choose to give you special directions geared to your needs or to a particular learning situation.

The material included in this program may be new to you, and you may want to continue your study of word attack skills further after you complete this program. If, however, this program is a review of skills you have previously learned, it will still help you to reinforce these skills.

Contents

1

Beginning, Middle, and Ending Consonants

Glossary

Vowels: the alphabet letters a, e, i, o, and u.
Consonants: all the other alphabet letters.
Graphemes: a printed symbol that is used to represent a speech sound.
Phonemes: the smallest unit of sound in a language, such as the b̲ in b̲oy.

Introduction

The English language has 26 letters — 21 *consonants* and 5 *vowels.* These letters, or *graphemes,* stand for sounds, or *phonemes.* The consonant letters stand for sounds when they go together with vowel letters to form words. This chapter will only deal with consonants. We will discuss vowels in Chapter 5.

In this chapter we will focus on the sounds that the consonant letters stand for at the beginning, middle, and end of words. You will be able to hear and know all these sounds. You will also learn to tell the difference between the sounds noted by the graphemes b̲ and p̲; f̲ and v̲; and t̲ and d̲.

Use Skilltape 1 to help you work through this chapter. The directions in this worktext will tell you when to turn on the skilltape.

The next section contains the pretests for Chapter 1. To see how much of this chapter you already know, go now to Pretests A and B. Complete both to the best of your ability.

Pretest A

Turn on Skilltape 1, side A.

Example: 𝓃

1. ____	6. ____	11. ____	16. ____
2. ____	7. ____	12. ____	17. ____
3. ____	8. ____	13. ____	18. ____
4. ____	9. ____	14. ____	19. ____
5. ____	10. ____	15. ____	20. ____

Pretest B

In this part of Pretest B, change the first consonant in each word to a different consonant to make a new word. Write the new word in the space provided.

Example: late *fate*

1. look_____   4. tip_____

2. cat_____   5. melt_____

3. fall_____   6. seal_____

In this part of the pretest, change the last consonant in each word to a different consonant to make a new word. Write the new word in the space provided.

Example: tin *tip*

7. pen_____   10. top_____

8. king_____   11. road_____

9. leak_____   12. flag_____

The following words have one or two letters underlined. In the space provided, write the consonant letter that stands for the sound you hear when you pronounce the word.

Example: trap _t_

13. supper_____   16. city_____

14. repeat_____   17. heaven_____

15. huddle_____   18. puzzle_____

Compare your answers to these pretests with those on page 16. Place a checkmark by each of your correct answers. Count the number correct for each pretest and write that number in the space provided here and on page 17.

> **Pretest A:** _____out of 20 correct
> **Pretest B:** _____out of 18 correct
> **Total:** _____out of 38 correct

If you got 34 or more correct, you can go on to the posttests on page 13.
If you got less than 34 correct, complete this chapter and then take the posttests.

Turn on the skilltape.

Table 1

Consonants and the Sounds They Represent

Introduction:
The letters in this table are single consonants. When they are *not* combined with other consonants, they almost all represent *one* sound whether they are found at the beginning, middle, or end of a word.

Turn on the skilltape.

Consonant	Beginning Sound	Middle Sound	Ending Sound
b	bed	stubble	stab
d	dog	radio	bread
f	fill	sniffle	leaf
h	horse	behold	(no sound)
j	job	object	(no sound)
k	king	broken	steak
l	love	miller	hill
m	moon	stomach	brim
n	nose	sinner	fin
p	pose	happy	map
r	room	hurry	hear
t	tooth	better	cut
v	vegetable	review	have
w	window	rewind	(no sound)
y	yet	beyond	(no sound)
z	zoo	dizzy	jazz

Consonants c, g, s, x, and q, not listed here, will be discussed in Chapter 2.

Exercise 1

In this exercise, the consonants you will be asked to name come at the beginning of the word.

Turn on the skilltape.

Example: *v*

1. *v*	6. *m*	11. *y*	16. *v*
2. *b*	7. *T*	12. *z*	17. *d*
3. *g*	8. *R*	13. *l*	18. *F*
4. *h*	9. *n*	14. *k*	19. *I*
5. *j*	10. *w*	15. *b*	20. *P*

Record the number of correct answers here and on page 17.

Exercise 1:   _____ out of 20 correct

Exercise 2

In this exercise change the beginning consonant in each word to make new words. Write as many new words as you can think of using the space provided. Say the words to yourself. Do the new words make sense? If not, leave them out. If you need help thinking of consonants, use Table 1 on page 5.

Example: _hat   mat, bat, vat, fat, pat, rat, cat, sat

1. _mast   _____

2. _taste   _____

3. _bite   _____

4. _silk   _____

5. _talk   _____

6. _bake   _____

7. _loose   _____

8. _lamp   _____

9. _best   _____

10. _paw   _____

Compare your answers with those given on page 15. Place a checkmark by those words that match.

If most of your answers were in the list of suggested answers, record your score on page 17 and go on to Exercise 3.

If two or more of your answers did not appear in the answer list and you can't find them in a dictionary, consult with your instructor.

Most of my answers matched those in the suggested answers: Yes____ No____

Exercise 3

In this exercise, you will be asked to pick out consonant sounds that come in the middle of the word.

Turn on the skilltape.

Example: _υ_

1. _v_	6. _l_	11. _d_	16. _b_
2. _w_	7. _h_	12. _y_	17. _p_
3. _t_	8. _F_	13. _m_	18. _f_
4. _t_	9. _p_	14. _l_	19. _n_
5. _h_	10. _k_	15. _v_	20. _m_

Record the number of correct answers here and on page 17.

Exercise 3: ____ out of 20 correct

Exercise 4

In this exercise, you are to pick out consonant sounds that come at the end of the word.

Turn on Skilltape 1, side B.

Example: _k_

1. _r_	6. _I_	11. _p_	16. _b_
2. _k_	7. _v_	12. _z_	17. _m_
3. _F_	8. _b_	13. _k_	18. _n_
4. _m_	9. _d_	14. _v_	19. _l_
5. _n_	10. _l_	15. _F_	20. _r_

Record the number of correct answers here and on page 17.

Exercise 4: _____ out of 20 correct

Exercise 5

In this exercise, change the final consonant in each word to make new words. Write these new words in the space provided below. There may be several choices. Write as many as you can. Say the words to yourself. Do the new words make sense? Are they familiar? If not, leave them out.

Example: real   *read, ream, reap, rear, real* _____

1. feed _____

2. worm _____

3. root _____

4. cut _____

5. frog _____

6. talk _____

7. part _____

8. fur _____

9. tab _____

10. grip _____

Compare your answers with those given on page 15. Place a checkmark by each of those words that match.

If most of your answers were in the list of suggested answers, record your score on page 17 and go on to page 9.

If two or more of your answers do not appear in the answer list and you can't find them in a dictionary, consult with your instructor.

Most of my answers matched those in the suggested answers: Yes _____   No _____

Sounds of P and B, V and F, D and T

There are several consonants which are alike in the way they are sounded. Some examples are *p* and *b* in the words *pat* and *bat*; *v* and *f* in *vat* and *fat,* and *d* and *t* in *had* and *hat.* Exercise 6 will help you to tell these consonant sounds apart.

Exercise 6

Part A

In Part A of this exercise, you will hear words containing the sounds represented by *p* and *b*. In the first space after each number below, write the letter that represents the sound you hear. Then put a checkmark in one of the three boxes to show whether you hear the sound at the beginning, middle, or end of the word.

Turn on the skilltape.

		Position		
	Sound	*Beginning*	*Middle*	*End*
Example	*p*	☐	☐	☑
1.	*p*	☐	☐	☑
2.	*p*	☑	☐	☐
3.	*b*	☐	☑	☐
4.	*b*	☑	☐	☐
5.	*p*	☐	☑	☐
6.	*b*	☐	☐	☑

Record the number of correct answers here and on page 17.

Exercise 6, Part A: _____ out of 12 correct

Part B

In Part B of this exercise, you will hear words containing the sounds of *f* and *v*.

Turn on the skilltape.

Sound		Position		
		Beginning	Middle	End
1. _F_	*grief*	☐	☐	☑
2. _v_	*vacuum*	☑	☐	☐
3. _F_	*feel*	☑	☐	☐
4. _v_	*solve*	☐	☐	☑
5. _F_	*suffer*	☐	☑	☐
6. _v_	*moving*	☐	☑	☐

Record the number of correct answers here and on page 17.

Exercise 6, Part B: _____ **out of 12 correct**

Part C

In Part C of this exercise you will hear words containing the sounds of *d* and *t*.

Turn on the skilltape.

Sound		Position		
		Beginning	Middle	End
1. _T_	*cost*	☐	☐	☑
2. _d_	*card*	☐	☐	☑
3. _T_	*heart*	☐	☐	☑
4. _d_	*hard*	☐	☐	☑
5. _T_	*patting*	☐	☑	☐
6. _d_	*padding*	☐	☑	☐

Record the number of correct answers here and on page 17.

Exercise 6, Part C: _____ **out of 12 correct**

Sounds of W and Y

The letters *w* and *y* are unusual, because they may be both consonants and vowels under different circumstances. We will discuss their use as vowels in Chapter 3, 4, 5 and 8. When *w* is a consonant, it sounds like the *w* in *wet*. When *y* is a consonant, it sounds like the *y* in *yes*. Exercises 7 and 8 will give you practice in hearing the sounds of *w* and *y* when they are consonants.

Exercise 7

Each of the following words contains the letter *w* or the letter *y*. Say each word to yourself. If you hear the consonant sound of *y* as in *yes* or *w* as in *wet*, write that letter in the space next to the word. If you do not hear either of those sounds, leave the space blank.

Example: want _𝓊_

1. cry_____
2. warm_𝓌_
3. bow_____
4. youth_𝓎_
5. walk_𝓌_

6. west_𝓌_
7. lady_____
8. yet_𝓎_
9. marry_____
10. saw_____

Compare your answers with those given on page 15. Place a checkmark by each of your correct answers. Count the number correct and record it here and on page 17.

Exercise 7: _____ out of 10 correct

Exercise 8

Turn on the skilltape.

In most cases, we find the consonant sounds *w* and *y* at the beginning of words like *was* and *yes*. But they may occur in the middle of words like *rewind* and *beyond*. In this exercise, if the *w* or *y* sound is at the beginning of a word, place the letter *w* or *y* in the first space in your worktext. If the sound is in the middle of a word, place the letter in the second space.

	Beginning	*Middle*
Example:	y	
1.	y	
2.		y
3.	w	
4.	w	
5.		w
6.	y	
7.		w
8.	y	y
9.	w	w
10.		

Record the number of correct answers here and on page 17.

Exercise 8: _____ out of 12 correct

Review Exercise

In this exercise, you will write the consonants you hear in each nonsense word.

Turn on the skilltape.

Example: kb

1. _____	6. _____	11. _____	16. _____
2. _____	7. _____	12. _____	17. _____
3. _____	8. _____	13. _____	18. _____
4. _____	9. _____	14. _____	19. _____
5. _____	10. _____	15. _____	20. _____

Record the number of correct answers here and on page 17.

Review Exercise: _____ out of 47 correct

Posttest A

Turn on the skilltape

Example: d

1. _p_
2. _b_
3. _m_
4. _r_
5. _m_
6. _f_

7. _t_
8. _d_
9. _b_
10. _t_
11. _v_
12. _s_

13. _n_
14. _v_
15. _k_
16. _p_
17. _s_
18. _f_

19. _w_
20. _y_
21. _y_
22. _w_
23. _w_

Posttest B

In this posttest, write a consonant letter in each blank below to make a known word. When you finish all the words, pronounce them to your instructor. There may be more than one choice. Read the example and then fill in the blanks below.

Example: ____ap becomes _t_ap

1. ____ork
2. hee____
3. bra____e
4. bul____
5. teache____
6. ____ack
7. ____ellow
8. ____est
9. law____er
10. ____ent

11. lea____
12. ____one
13. be____ide
14. see____
15. ____andwich
16. ____ictory
17. ____undred
18. ____owl
19. ____outh
20. re____eat

Compare your answers to these posttests with those on page 16. Place a checkmark by each of your correct answers. Count the number correct for each posttest and record your score here and on page 17.

Posttest A: ____ out of 23 correct
Posttest B: ____ out of 20 correct
Total: ____ out of 43 correct

If you got 39 or more correct, you can go on to the next chapter and take the pretests as directed.

If you got less than 39 correct, talk with your instructor.

Show your instructor the summary sheet on page 17 on which you have recorded your scores for all the exercises and tests.

Answers to Exercises Not on the Skilltape

Exercise 2

1. fast, last, vast, cast, past
2. paste, waste, haste, baste, caste
3. kite, rite, site, mite, cite
4. milk, bilk
5. walk, balk

6. make, fake, lake, rake, wake, cake, sake, take
7. moose, goose, noose
8. camp, damp, ramp, vamp, tamp,
9. jest, hest, gest, lest, nest, pest, zest, rest, test, vest, west
10. jaw, law, raw, maw, caw, saw, haw, yaw

Exercise 5

1. feel, feet
2. work, word, worn
3. room, roof, rook, rood
4. cub, cup, cur, cud, cuff, cull, cuss
5. from

6. tall,
7. park
8. fun, full, fuss
9. tag, tap, tad, tan, tar, tall, tam, tat, tax
10. grid, grim, grin, grit, grill

Exercise 7

2. w   4. y   5. w   6. w   8. y

Exercise 8

1. y, middle
2. y, middle
3. y, beginning
4. w, beginning
5. w, beginning

6. w, middle
7. y, beginning
8. w, middle
9. y, beginning and middle
10. w, beginning and middle

Answers to Pretests and Posttests

Pretest A

1. p	6. f	11. z	16. p
2. b	7. t	12. v	17. s
3. m	8. d	13. v	18. f
4. r	9. j or g	14. n	19. v
5. m	10. t	15. k	20. y

Pretest B

You should be able to find your answers here or in a dictionary, if they are correct.

1. book, took, nook, cook, gook, hook, kook, rook
2. bat, sat, mat, fat, hat, pat, rat, tat, vat
3. tall, ball, mall, call, gall, hall, pall, wall
4. sip, nip, lip, dip, hip, kip, pip, rip, yip, zip
5. pelt, felt, belt, celt, welt
6. meal, veal, weal, zeal, real, deal, heal, peal, teal
7. pet, ped, peg, pep, pew
8. kind, kink
9. leap, lean, lead, leaf
10. tot, ton, tog, tor, tow, toy
11. roam, roan, roar
12. flap, flat, flab, flak, flam, flax, flay
13. p
14. p
15. d
16. t
17. v
18. z

Posttest A

1. p	7. t	13. n	19. v
2. b	8. d	14. v	20. y
3. m	9. b	15. k	21. y
4. r	10. t	16. p	22. w
5. m	11. v	17. s	23. w
6. f	12. z	18. f	

Posttest B

You should be able to find your answers here or in a dictionary, if they are correct.

1. fork, cork, pork
2. heel, heed
3. brace, brake, brave
4. bull, bulk, bulb
5. teacher, teaches
6. back, rack, sack, lack, mack, hack, jack, pack, tack
7. yellow, mellow, bellow, fellow
8. west, best, gest, nest, zest, vest, test, rest, hest, jest, lest, pest
9. lawyer
10. sent, went, lent, dent, gent, sent, rent, tent, bent, vent
11. leaf, lead, leak, lean, leap
12. cone, gone, hone, lone, bone, done, none, pone, tone, zone
13. beside, betide
14. seen, seem, seed, seek, seep, sear
15. sandwich
16. victory
17. hundred
18. bowl, cowl, fowl, howl, jowl, yowl
19. mouth, south, couth, youth
20. repeat, reheat, reseat

SUMMARY SHEET

Chapter 1

Record your scores for each test and exercise.

	Number Correct	**Instructor's Comments**
Pretest A	_____ out of 20 correct	
Pretest B	_____ out of 18 correct	
Exercise 1	_____ out of 20 correct	
Exercise 2	Most of my answers matched those in the list of suggested answers: Yes _____ No _____	
Exercise 3	_____ out of 20 correct	
Exercise 4	_____ out of 20 correct	
Exercise 5	Most of my answers matched those in the list of suggested answers: Yes _____ No _____	
Exercise 6		
Part A	_____ out of 12 correct	
Part B	_____ out of 12 correct	
Part C	_____ out of 12 correct	
Exercise 7	_____ out of 10 correct	
Exercise 8	_____ out of 12 correct	
Review Exercise	_____ out of 47 correct	
Posttest A	_13_ out of 23 correct	
Posttest B	_____ out of 20 correct	

2

Confusing
Consonants

Glossary

Confusing Consonants: those consonants which represent more than one sound.

Silent Consonants: those consonants which do not represent a sound in words.

Nonsense Words: words which have no meaning.

Introduction

Chapter 1 covered those consonants that stand for only one sound found at the beginning, middle, or end of words. The letter *b* for example, always stands for the same sound whether it is at the beginning (bag), in the middle (stubble), or at the end of a word (stab).

In this chapter, you will learn about the consonants that stand for *more* than one sound. You will also come to recognize when a word has a consonant that is silent. This chapter will help you recognize words which have the consonant *q*. Finally, when you have completed this chapter, you will be able to tell the different sounds noted by the consonants *c, g, s,* and *x*.

Use Skilltape 2 to help you work through this chapter. The directions in this worktext will tell you when to turn on the skilltape.

The next section contains the pretests for Chapter 2. To see how much of the material in this chapter you already know, go now to Pretests A and B. Complete both just as well as you can.

Pretest A

Turn on the Skilltape 2, side A.

Example: 𝒈

1. ___	6. ___	11. ___	16. ___	21. ___
2. ___	7. ___	12. ___	17. ___	22. ___
3. ___	8. ___	13. ___	18. ___	23. ___
4. ___	9. ___	14. ___	19. ___	24. ___
5. ___	10. ___	15. ___	20. ___	25. ___

Pretest B

Example: brought

1. knee
2. wrong
3. debt
4. dumb
5. sign
6. puzzle

7. pneumonia
8. sight
9. spell
10. gnat
11. patch
12. talk

Record the number of correct answers here and on page 46.

Pretest A: ___out of 25 correct
Pretest B: ___out of 13 correct
Total: ___out of 38 correct

If you got 34 or more correct, you may go on to the posttests on pages 39–41.
If you got less than 34 correct, complete this chapter and then take the posttests.

The Two Sounds of C

Exercise 1

Turn on the skilltape.

Example: *k̸*

1. ___	6. ___
2. ___	7. ___
3. ___	8. ___
4. ___	9. ___
5. ___	10. ___

Record the number of correct answers here and on page 46.

Exercise 1:   ___out of 10 correct

Exercise 2

You may have noticed that the hard sound represented by the letter *c* sounds like *k* whereas the soft sound represented by *c* sounds like *s*. *C* represents either the sound of *k* or of *s*. It represents no sound of its own.

Look at the following list of words. Write *s* in the space to the right of the word if the *c* sound at the beginning of the word is like an *s* or *k* if the *c* sounds like a *k*. Here is an example with the *c* representing a *k* sound.

Example: corn *k̸*

1. canal___ *K*	6. candle___ *k*
2. coward___ *k*	7. cylinder___ *S*
3. cedar___ *S*	8. cough___ *k*
4. coin___ *k*	9. cider___ *S*
5. circus___ *S*	10. center___ *S*

Compare your answers with those given on page 42. Place a checkmark by each of your correct answers. Count the number correct and record that number here and on page 46.

Exercise 2:   ___out of 10 correct

Exercise 3

Turn on the skilltape.

Example: *R*

1. ___	6. ___
2. ___	7. ___
3. ___	8. ___
4. ___	9. ___
5. ___	10. ___

Record the number of correct answers here and on page 46.

Exercise 3: ___out of 10 correct

Exercise 4

In the following words, the letter *c* is found in the middle of the word. In the space to the right of each word, indicate whether the *c* is hard (by writing the letter *k*) or soft (by writing the letter *s*).

Example: uncle *R*

1. cycle _s_	6. circle _s_
2. circus _s_	7. dancing _s_
3. cyclone _s_	8. mercy _s_
4. Nancy _s_	9. bacon _k_
5. cancel _k_	10. escape _k_

Compare your answers with those given on page 42. Place a checkmark by each of your correct answers. Count the number correct and record that number here and on page 46.

Exercise 4: ___out of 10 correct

Exercise 5

Turn on the skilltape.

Example: _k_

1. ____   6. ____

2. ____   7. ____

3. ____   8. ____

4. ____   9. ____

5. ____   10. ____

Record the number of correct answers here and on page 46.

Exercise 5:   ____ out of 10 correct

Exercise 6

In the following words, the sound which *c* represents will be found at the end of the word. In the word *race,* the sound which *c* represents is an *s* (soft) sound. In the word *comic,* the sound which both *c*'s represent is a *k* (hard) sound. Write *s* or *k* for each word below to show the sound at the end of each word. An example is done for you.

Example: produce _s_

1. reduce _s_   6. atomic _k_

2. plastic _k_   7. piece _s_

3. ounce _s_   8. chance _s_

4. rejoice _s_   9. tactic _k_

5. electric _k_   10. voice _s_

Compare your answers with those given on page 42. Place a checkmark by each of your correct answers. Count the number correct and record that number here and on page 46.

Exercise 6:   ____ out of 10 correct

More About the Sound of C

In all the previous exercises, the sound of *c* was either soft like an *s* sound or hard like a *k* sound. Have you noticed any pattern that determines when the sound of *c* is hard or soft?

If you look carefully, you will see that when the letter *c* is followed by the letters *e, i,* or *y,* the *c* has the sound of *s.* In all other cases, the letter *c* will represent a hard *k* sound. In Table 1 you will find some words which show this rule.

Table 1

The Rule for C

cell	recite	In this list, the letter *c* in each word represents the soft *s* sound. Notice the letters *e, i,* or *y* follow the *c.*
dance	spicy	
cereal	city	
cinder		

coin	decade	In this list, the letter *c* in each word represents the hard *k* sound. Notice that any letter except *e, i,* or *y* make the sound of *c* hard. In most cases when a word ends in *c,* the *c* will be hard.
atomic	clean	
canal	act	
cot	cut	

cyclone	Notice that this list has words with both the hard and soft sounds of *c* in them.
cycle	
circus	
circle	

Exercise 7

Here is a list of nonsense words. Using the rule you just learned, decide in each case whether the letter *c* represents a hard sound or a soft sound. Write *s* (soft) or *k* (hard) in the space to the right of the "word" to show the sound. An example is done for you.

Example: ceple ___s___

1. cen___s___   6. clin___k___
2. cyl___s___   7. trac___k___
3. cas___k___   8. ract___k___
4. ced___s___   9. foce___s___
5. cit___s___   10. lacon___k___

Compare your answers with those given on page 42. Place a checkmark by each of your correct answers. Count the number correct and record that number here and on page 46.

Exercise 7:   _____out of 10 correct

The Two Sounds of G

Exercise 8

Turn on the skilltape.

Example: _g_

1. _____   6. _____
2. _____   7. _____
3. _____   8. _____
4. _____   9. _____
5. _____   10. _____

Record the number of correct answers here and on page 46.

Exercise 8:   _____out of 10 correct

Exercise 9

You have heard that the hard sound of the letter *g* sounds like the *g* in *goat,* whereas the soft sound of *g* sounds like a *j,* as in gym. The letter *g* represents either its own sound or the sound of *j.*

   In the following list, the letter *g* is underlined in each word. As before, write *g* on the line if the underlined *g* represents a hard sound or *j* if the sound is soft.

1. geography___*j*___
2. gone___*g*___
3. good___*g*___
4. gay___*g*___
5. giant___*j*___

6. gypsy___*j*___
7. gum___*g*___
8. gym___*j*___
9. game___*g*___
10. George___*j*___ ___*j*___

Compare your answers with those given on page 42. Place a checkmark by each of your correct answers. Count the number correct and record that number here and on page 46. Number 10 counts as two correct answers.

Exercise 9:   _____out of 11 correct

Exercise 10

Turn on Skilltape 2, side B.

Example: *g j*

1. _____
2. _____
3. _____
4. _____
5. _____

6. _____
7. _____
8. _____
9. _____
10. _____

Record the number of correct answers here and on page 46.

Exercise 10:   _____out of 10 correct

Exercise 11

In this exercise, you will hear the letter *g* in the middle of the words. Read each word aloud. In the space provided, show whether the *g* is hard (by writing the letter *g*) or soft (by writing the letter *j*). An example is done for you.

Example: logger *g*

1. sugar *g*
2. magic *j*
3. agree *g*
4. tiger *g*
5. again *g*

6. organ *g*
7. danger *j*
8. imagine *j*
9. begun *g*
10. energy *j*

Compare your answers with those given on page 42. Place a checkmark by each of your correct answers. Count the number correct and record that number here and on page 46.

Exercise 11: _____out of 10 correct

Exercise 12

Turn on the skilltape.

Example: *j*

1. ____
2. ____
3. ____
4. ____
5. ____

6. ____
7. ____
8. ____
9. ____
10. ____

Record the number of correct answers here and on page 46.

Exercise 12: _____out of 10 correct

Exercise 13

In this exercise, the sound which *g* represents is found at the end of the words. For example, in the word *stage*, the sound which *g* represents is a *j* or soft sound. In the word *brag*, the sound of *g* is hard. These words are used as examples below. For the remainng ten words, write *g* or *j* after each word to show whether the sound of *g* at the end is hard or soft. Two examples are done for you.

Examples: stage___*j*___   brag___*g*___

1. edge___*j*___
2. page___*j*___
3. bug___*g*___
4. drag___*g*___
5. age___*j*___

6. bridge___*j*___
7. charge___*j*___
8. voyage___*j*___
9. badge___*j*___
10. rig___*g*___

Compare your answers with those given on page 42. Place a checkmark by each of your correct answers. Count the number correct and record that number here and on page 46.

Exercise 13:   _____ out of 10 correct

More About the Sound of G

In all the previous exercises, the sound of *g* was either soft like a *j* sound or hard like the *g* in *go*. Have you noticed any pattern that determines when the sound of *g* is hard or soft?

If you look carefully, you will see that when the letter *g* is followed by the letters *e, i,* or *y,* the *g* has the sound of *j*. (There are a few exceptions to this rule, and they will be discussed later in the chapter.) In most other cases, the letter *g* will be hard. This rule is the same as for the sounds of *c*. In Table 2, you will find some words which show this rule.

Table 2

Rules for G

char**g**e	**g**iant
gem	**g**ymnast
gentle	ma**g**ic
fud**g**e	**g**in**g**er
pa**g**e	colle**g**e

In this list, the letter *g* in each word represents the soft *j* sound. Notice that these words follow the rule about *g* before the letters *e*, *i*, or *y*.

smu**g**	**g**row
game	**g**allop
goat	**g**ather
guard	**g**ust
gleam	**g**rape

In this list, the letter *g* in each word represents the hard sound. Notice that any letters other than *e*, *i*, or *y* make the sound of *g* hard. In most cases when a word ends in *g*, the *g* will be hard.

gor**g**e
gara**g**e
gau**g**e

Notice that in this list each word has both the hard and soft sounds of *g*.

Exercise 14

Here is a list of nonsense words. Determine if the letter *g* in each word represents a hard sound or a soft (j) sound. Write *g* or *j* in the space provided. Here is an example:

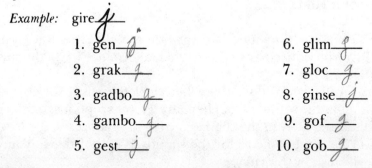

Example: gire *j*

1. gen __*j*__
2. grak __*j*__
3. gadbo __*g*__
4. gambo __*g*__
5. gest __*j*__

6. glim __*g*__
7. gloc __*g*__
8. ginse __*j*__
9. gof __*g*__
10. gob __*g*__

Compare your answers with those given on page 42. Place a checkmark by each of your correct answers. Count the number correct and record that number here and on page 46.

Exercise 14: _____ out of 10 correct

Exceptions to the Rule for G

The rule for the sound of *g* when followed by *e, i,* or *y* has some exceptions. In the following list of words, *g* has a hard sound, even though it is followed by *e* or *i*.

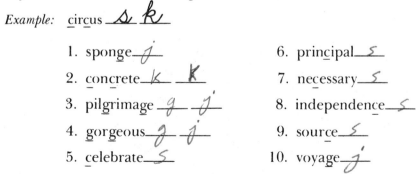

g̲eese	g̲ive
g̲et	g̲irl
g̲ears	g̲irdle
tar̲g̲et	g̲ift
ti̲g̲er	g̲ilt
an̲g̲er	be̲g̲in

When you are faced with an unfamiliar word which has a *g* followed by *e, i,* or *y,* try both the hard and soft sound. Whichever sounds most familiar will probably be correct. If in doubt, consult your dictionary.

Review Exercise

In this exercise, decide whether the underlined sound(s) in each word below is a hard or soft *c,* or a hard or soft *g.* In the space provided, write the letter for the sound which the underlined letter makes. For example, in the word "ci̲r̲cus" the first *c* is soft and has an *s* sound while the second *c* is hard and has a *k* sound. In "gorge," the first *g* is hard and has the *g* sound, while the second *g* is soft and has the *j* sound. Use the letters *s* and *k, g* and *j* to show the sounds of *c* and *g.*

Example: ci̲r̲cus *s k*

1. spon̲g̲e *j*
2. c̲on̲c̲rete *k   k*
3. pil̲g̲rima̲g̲e *g   j*
4. g̲or̲g̲eous *g   j*
5. c̲elebrate *s*

6. prin̲c̲ipal *s*
7. ne̲c̲essary *s*
8. independen̲c̲e *s*
9. sour̲c̲e *s*
10. voya̲g̲e *j*

Compare your answers with those given on page 43. Place a checkmark by each of your correct answers. Count the number correct, and record that number here and on page 46.

Review Exercise: _____ **out of 13 correct**

The Two Sounds of S

Turn on the skilltape.

Exercise 15

Example: praise _𝒵_

1. ____   6. ____
2. ____   7. ____
3. ____   8. ____
4. ____   9. ____
5. ____   10. ____

Record the number of correct answers here an on page 46.

Exercise 15: ____ out of 10 correct

Exercise 16

In the following list of words, the letter *s* is underlined. Determine whether the *s* represents an *s* or a *z* sound. In the space provided, write the letter for the sound, either an *s* or a *z*. An example is done for you.

Example: floss _𝒮_

1. fuse____   6. germs____
2. his____   7. whistle____
3. fussy____   8. listen____
4. sidewalk____   9. goes____
5. jumps____   10. chairs____

Compare your answers with those given on page 43. Place a checkmark by each of your correct answers. Count the number correct and record that number here and on page 46.

Exercise 16: ____ out of 10 correct

Vowels, Plurals, and the Letter S

In the following list of words, notice that there is an *s* sound in each word.

<u>s</u>nake	mi<u>ss</u>ile
<u>s</u>it	<u>s</u>leep
<u>s</u>unny	wre<u>st</u>le
<u>s</u>kim	my<u>st</u>ery
unle<u>ss</u>	<u>s</u>incere

In the next list of words, notice that there is a *z* sound in each word.

spire<u>s</u>	her<u>s</u>
plane<u>s</u>	ro<u>s</u>e
bu<u>s</u>y	fu<u>s</u>e
churche<u>s</u>	mi<u>s</u>er
sale<u>s</u>	blend<u>s</u>

Generally, it may be said that when plural words end in *s,* the *s* will sound like a *z* (sale<u>s</u>).

In many words when the *s* is found between two vowels, (fu<u>s</u>e) the *s* represents a *z* sound. Also, in many small words (hi<u>s</u>, her<u>s</u>), the *s* represents a *z* sound. In most other cases the *s* represents an *s* sound.

Special Sounds

Turn on the skilltape.

Exercise 17

Example: clo<u>s</u>ure

1. measure

2. pleasure

3. pressure

4. fissure

5. assure

Compare your answers with those given on page 43. Place a checkmark by each of your correct answers. Count the number correct and record that number here and on page 46.

Exercise 17:   _____out of 5 correct

Exercise 18

As you listen to the tape, write *z*, *gz*, or *ks* in the space provided.

Turn on the skilltape.

Example: fix *ks*

1. xylem_____

2. exist_____

3. examine_____

4. excite_____

5. excel_____

6. exact_____

7. excuse_____

8. example_____

9. xenon_____

10. exclude_____

Compare your answers with those given on page 43. Place a checkmark by each of your correct answers. Count the number correct and record that number here and on page 46.

Exercise 18:   _____out of 10 correct

Exercise 19

Turn on the skilltape.

Example: q<u>u</u>iz

1. quick	6. quilt
2. question	7. quinine
3. quiet	8. request
4. quota	9. require
5. quiver	10. misquote

If you have followed the directions to underline every *qu*, you may record your score here and on page 46 as 10 out of 10 correct.

Exercise 19:   ——out of 10 correct

Silent Consonants

Another aspect of confusing consonants is "silent" or unpronounced consonants. These consonants make it very difficult to spell and sound out unknown words. However, in spite of this difficulty, there are several patterns which will help you to sound out many words more easily.

Table 3 contains words with the most frequently silent letters.

Table 3

Frequently Silent Consonants

Beginning Silent Letters	*Middle or Ending Silent Letters*
Frequent — wrong	Frequent — comb
know	match, watch
scene	badge
Infrequent — gnaw	rhythm
honor	light
psychology	sign
pneumonia	listen
	Infrequent — debt
	walk
	calf

Exercise 20

Using Table 3 as a guide, cross out the silent consonant(s) in the following words. Then pronounce the word to yourself. An example is done for you.

Example: thum~~b~~

1. num~~b~~
2. ~~w~~rench
3. ~~k~~nelt
4. ma~~t~~ch
5. ~~g~~nome

6. ~~s~~cent
7. lis~~t~~en
8. mi~~gh~~t
9. bri~~d~~ge
10. tal~~k~~

Compare your answers with those given on page 43. Place a checkmark by each of your correct answers. Count the number correct and record that number here and on page 46.

Exercise 20: _____ out of 11 correct

Exercise 21

In this exercise, insert the silent consonant (or consonants) missing in each word. Then pronounce each word to yourself. The consonants you select should be *silent.* Read the example and begin. Remember: the letters you inserted are silent consonants and do not affect the pronunciation of the word.

Example: ba*l*k

1. hi_g_ _h_
2. pi_t_ch
3. e_d_ge
4. _w_rote
5. lu_c_k

6. crum_b_
7. _k_nife
8. ha_l_f
9. whis_t_le
10. si_g_n

Compare your answers with those given on page 43. Place a checkmark by each of your correct answers. Count the number correct and record that number here and on page 46.

Exercise 21: _____ out of 11 correct

Words with Silent Letters

The following lists contain the most common words that have silent letters.

List 1

Words with Double Consonants

When two consonants come together in a word and are alike, as in "letter," the first consonant is pronounced and the second is silent. Note the following examples:

litt̸le	prett̸y
sil̸ly	supp̸er
puz̸zle	bal̸loon
ridd̸le	bott̸le

List 2

Words with Silent b

climb̸	comb̸
lamb̸	doub̸t
thumb̸	deb̸t

List 3

Words with Silent w̸

w̸rap	w̸ring
w̸rong	w̸retch
w̸rist	w̸rote
w̸rite	w̸ren

List 4

Words with Silent t

list̸en	rust̸le
fast̸en	hust̸le
moist̸en	whist̸le

List 5

Words with Silent g or k

gnash	knelt
gnat	knee
gnaw	knock
knife	knight
knob	knew

List 6

Words with Silent gh

knight	thought
eight	thigh
delight	right
sleigh	straight
slight	night
sigh	fight

List 7

Words with Silent -c(k)

stick	track
black	ticket
sick	thicket

List 8

Words with Silent -t(ch)

catch	watch
pitch	ditch
hitch	stitch
match	

List 9

Words with Silent -d(ge)

fudge	budge
badge	judge
ridge	midget
bridge	dredge

Posttest A

For the following words, show whether the consonant *c* represents an *s* sound by writing *s* or a *k* sound by writing *k* in the space provided.

Example: crane __*k*__

1. cancel __k__ __s__
2. recent __s__
3. grocer __s__
4. actor __k__
5. princess __s__

6. furnace __s__
7. panic __k__
8. picnic __k__ __k__
9. piece __s__
10. doctor __k__

Posttest B

For the following words, show whether the consonant *g* represents a *g* sound by writing *g* or *j* sound by writing *j* in the space provided.

Example: gumption __*g*__

1. agent __j__
2. golden __g__
3. engine __j__
4. giraffe __j__
5. begin __g__

6. magazine __g__
7. geese __g__
8. pigeon __j__
9. green __g__
10. sugar __g__

Posttest C

For the following words, show whether the consonant *s* represents an *s* sound by writing *s* or a *z* sound by writing *z* in the space provided.

Example: peas __*z*__

1. colleges __z__
2. single __s__

3. because __z__
4. measles __z__ __z__

5. this___s___   8. inside___s___

6. rose___z___   9. sound___s___

7. reside___z___   10. causes___z___ ___z___

Posttest D

For these nonsense words, write whether the underlined consonant represents the sound of *s, k, g, j,* or *z* in the space provided.

Example: pag___g___

1. cyder___s___	6. bes___s___	11. cipter___s___	16. gyng___j___
2. gorb___g___	7. pinge___j___	12. bise___s___	17. rimic___k___
3. cag___k___	8. brince___s___	13. gand___g___	18. gyst___j___
4. lils___z___	9. gern___j___	14. precel___s___	19. clob___k___
5. cenal___k___	10. coprin___k___	15. recom___k___	20. sinter___s___

Posttest E

Listed below are 15 words. All the words have at least one silent consonant. *Some* have *more* than one. Cross out the silent consonant(s) in each word.

Example: plumb̸

numb̸	g̸nash	fas̸ten
cas̸tle	k̸not	mois̸ten
comb̸	w̸restle	but̸cher
g̸nome	deb̸t	pit̸cher
w̸reck̸	w̸ren	g̸nat

Posttest F

Listed below are ten nonsense words. By using the knowledge you have gained, cross out the silent consonants as you did in Posttest E.

wras   simb   deght

dobt   bodge   prosten

gneb   seck   knib

zotch

Compare your answers to these posttests with those on page 44–45. Place a checkmark by each of your correct answers. Count the number correct for each posttest and record your score here and on page 46.

Posttest A: _12_ out of 12 **corrct**
Posttest B: _9_ out of 10 **correct**
Posttest C: _11_ out of 12 **correct**
Posttest D: _17_ out of 21 **correct**
Posttest E: _16_ out of 17 **correct**
Posttest F: _11_ out of 11 **correct**
Total: _76_ out of 83 **correct**

If you got 75 or more correct, you can go on to the next chapter and take the pretests as directed.

If you got less than 75 correct, talk with your instructor.

Show your instructor the summary sheet on page 46 on which you have recorded your scores for all the exercises and tests.

Answers to Exercises Not on the Skilltape

Exercise 2

1. k	4. k	7. s	10. s
2. k	5. s	8. k	
3. s	6. k	9. s	

Exercise 4

1. k	4. s	7. s	10. k
2. k	5. s	8. s	
3. k	6. k	9. k	

Exercise 6

1. s	4. s	7. s	10. s
2. k	5. k	8. s	
3. s	6. k	9. k	

Exercise 7

1. s	4. s	7. k	10. k
2. s	5. s	8. k	
3. k	6. k	9. s	

Exercise 9

1. j	4. g	7. g	10. j, j
2. g	5. j	8. j	
3. g	6. j	9. g	

Exercise 11

1. g	4. g	7. j	10. j
2. j	5. g	8. j	
3. g	6. g	9. g	

Exercise 13

1. j	4. g	7. j	10. g
2. j	5. j	8. j	
3. g	6. j	9. j	

Exercise 14

1. j	4. g	7. g	10. g
2. g	5. j	8. j	
3. g	6. g	9. g	

Review Exercise

1. j	4. g,j	7. s	10. j
2. k, k	5. s	8. s	
3. g,j	6. s	9. s	

Exercise 16

1. z	4. s	7. s	10. z
2. z	5. s	8. s	
3. s	6. z	9. z	

Exercise 17

You should have underlined all the *s*'s in the five words.

Exercise 18

1. z	4. ks	7. ks	10. ks
2. gz	5. ks	8. gz	
3. gz	6. gz	9. z	

Exercise 20

1. b	4. t	7. t	10. l
2. w	5. g	8. g, h	
3. k	6. s	9. d	

Exercise 21

1. g, h	4. w	7. k	10. g
2. t	5. c	8. l	
3. d	6. b	9. t	

Answers to Pretests and Posttests

Pretest A

1. z	8. x (ks)	15. k	22. z
2. s	9. k	16. g	23. z
3. g	10. k	17. k	24. s
4. j	11. s	18. g	25. z
5. g	12. j	19. s	
6. s	13. g	20. k	
7. s	14. s	21. s	

Pretest B

1. knee	4. dumb	7. pneumonia	10. gnat
2. wrong	5. sign	8. sight	11. patch
3. debt	6. puzzle	9. spell	12. talk

Posttest A

1. k, s	4. k	7. k	10. k
2. s	5. s	8. k, k	
3. s	6. s	9. s	

Posttest B

1. j	4. j	7. g	10. g
2. g	5. g	8. j	
3. j	6. g	9. g	

Posttest C

1. z	4. z, z	7. z	10. z, z
2. s	5. s	8. s	
3. z	6. z	9. s	

Posttest D

1. s	6. s	11. s	16. j, g
2. g	7. j	12. z	17. k
3. k	8. s	13. g	18. j
4. z	9. j	14. s	19. k
5. s	10. k	15. k	20. s

Posttest E

numb	knot	butcher	wreck
gnash	moisten	gnome	wren
fasten	comb	debt	gnat
castle	wrestle	pitcher	

Posttest F

wras	dobt	gneb	zotch
simb	bodge	seck	
deght	prosten	knib	

SUMMARY SHEET

Chapter 2

Record your scores for each test and exercise.

	Number Correct	Instructor's Comments
Pretest A	_____out of 25 correct	
Pretest B	_____out of 13 correct	
Exercise 1	_____out of 10 correct	
Exercise 2	_____out of 10 correct	
Exercise 3	_____out of 10 correct	
Exercise 4	_____out of 10 correct	
Exercise 5	_____out of 10 correct	
Exercise 6	_____out of 10 correct	
Exercise 7	_____out of 10 correct	
Exercise 8	_____out of 10 correct	
Exercise 9	_____out of 11 correct	
Exercise 10	_____out of 10 correct	
Exercise 11	_____out of 10 correct	
Exercise 12	_____out of 10 correct	
Exercise 13	_____out of 10 correct	
Exercise 14	_____out of 10 correct	
Review Exercise	_____out of 13 correct	
Exercise 15	_____out of 10 correct	
Exercise 16	_____out of 10 correct	
Exercise 17	_____out of 5 correct	
Exercise 18	_____out of 10 correct	
Exercise 19	_____out of 10 correct	
Exercise 20	_____out of 11 correct	
Exercise 21	_____out of 11 correct	
Posttest A	_____out of 12 correct	
Posttest B	_____out of 10 correct	
Posttest C	_____out of 12 correct	
Posttest D	_____out of 21 correct	
Posttest E	_____out of 17 correct	
Posttest F	_____out of 11 correct	

3

Consonant
Blends

Glossary

Consonant Blends: a grouping of two or three consonants in which each consonant represents its own sound and you can hear each sound.

Introduction

In Chapters, 1 and 2 you learned that consonants come at the beginning, middle, and end of words. There are many words in our language which have two or three consonants that are grouped together, such as the words *blue, split, snake,* and *task.* These groups of consonants are called *consonant blends.* This chapter will help you hear and know consonant blends at the beginning and end of words.

Use Skilltape 3 to help you work through this chapter. The directions in this worktext will tell you when to turn on the skilltape.

The next section is the pretests for Chapter 3. To see how much of the material in this chapter you already know, go now to Pretests A, B, and C. Complete each to the best of your ability.

Pretest A

Turn on Skilltape 3, side A.

Example: _ll_

1. ___	6. ___	11. ___	16. ___
2. ___	7. ___	12. ___	17. ___
3. ___	8. ___	13. ___	18. ___
4. ___	9. ___	14. ___	19. ___
5. ___	10. ___	15. ___	20. ___

Pretest B

Example: _lp_

1. ___	6. ___	11. ___
2. ___	7. ___	12. ___
3. ___	8. ___	13. ___
4. ___	9. ___	14. ___
5. ___	10. ___	15. ___

Pretest C

Example: _scr_

1. ___
2. ___
3. ___
4. ___

Compare your answers to these pretests with those on page 63. Place a checkmark by each of your correct answers. Count the number correct for each pretest and write that number in the space provided here and on page 64.

Pretest A: _____out of 20 correct
Pretest B: _____out of 15 correct
Pretest C: _____out of 4 correct
  Total: _____out of 39 correct

If you got 35 or more correct, you may go on to the posttests on pages 60–61.
If you got less than 35 correct, complete this chapter and then take the posttests.

The S Blends

Exercise 1

In this exercise, the consonant blends you will name come at the beginning of the word.

Turn on the skilltape.

Example: _st_

1. _sc_	6. _sp_	11. _sn_	16. _sp_
2. _st_	7. _sw_	12. _sk_	17. _sc_
3. _sl_	8. _sp_	13. _sk_	18. _sw_
4. _sp_	9. _sn_	14. _sl_	19. _st_
5. _sk_	10. _sm_	15. _sn_	20. _sm_

Record the number of correct answers here and on page 64.

Exercise 1: _19_ **out of 20 correct**

Exercise 2

In this exercise, replace the first consonant in each word with a consonant blend beginning with the letter *s*. Write the new word in the space provided. Use the following blends: sp, st, sk, sw, sn, sc, sm, sl. There may be one or more choices.

Example: tell _spell_

1. nice _slice / spice_
   sly 2. by _sky / spy / sty_
3. team _steam_
   sting 4. ring _swing / sling_
5. mow _snow / slow / stow_
6. ball _small / stall_ snore
7. more _score / store / swore_
8. made _slade / spade_
9. make _snake / stake_
10. dare _spare / snare / scare_

Compare your answers with those given on page 62. Place a checkmark by each of your correct answers. Count the number correct and record that number here and on page 64.

Exercise 2: ____ **out of 10 correct**

The R Blends

Exercise 3

In this exercise, the consonant blends you will name come at the beginning of the word. These consonant blends all have *r* as their second letter.

Turn on the skilltape.

<u>br</u>ead, <u>cr</u>y, <u>dr</u>ink, <u>fr</u>om,

<u>gr</u>ow, <u>pr</u>op, <u>tr</u>y

Example: gr

1. ___	6. ___	11. ___
2. ___	7. ___	12. ___
3. ___	8. ___	13. ___
4. ___	9. ___	14. ___
5. ___	10. ___	15. ___

Record the number of correct answers here and on page 64.

Exercise 3: ___out of 15 correct

Exercise 4

For this exercise, select an appropriate blend that will form a word when placed in the blank. Then pronounce the word to yourself.

Example: tr, gr, dr *tr*ain

1. gr, br, tr ___and
2. gr, tr, fr ___ap
3. pr, br, dr ___ing
4. dr, cr, gr ___inge
5. fr, dr, br ___eam

6. gr, fr, dr ___esh
7. gr, tr, cr ___asp
8. dr, pr, br ___ice
9. br, gr, dr ___op
10. cr, dr, fr ___owd

Compare your answers with those given on page 62. Place a checkmark by each of your correct answers. Count the number correct and record that number here and on page 64.

Exercise 4: ___out of 10 correct

The L Blends

Exercise 5

In this exercise, the consonant blends you will name come at the beginning of the word. All these consonant blends have *l* as their second letter. Note the following words: blend, clown, flipped, glow, plow, sliver.

Turn on the skilltape.

Example: *cl*

1. ___	6. ___	11. ___
2. ___	7. ___	12. ___
3. ___	8. ___	13. ___
4. ___	9. ___	14. ___
5. ___	10. ___	15. ___

Record the number of correct answers here and on page 64.

Exercise: ___ **out of 15 correct**

Exercise 6

For this exercise select one blend from the three in each question that will form a word when placed in the blank. Then pronounce the word to yourself.

Example: sl, pl, bl *bl*ock

1. pl, cl, gl ___ock
2. sl, pl, cl ___ed
3. fl, bl, pl ___ane
4. cl, gl, sl ___obe
5. fl, cl, bl ___at

6. bl, pl, gl ___ay
7. gl, sl, bl ___ank
8. cl, pl, gl ___own
9. bl, sl, cl ___ide
10. cl, gl, pl ___ip

Compare your answers with those given on page 62. Place a checkmark by each of your correct answers. Count the number correct and record that number here and on page 64.

Exercise 6: ___ **out of 10 correct**

The W Blends

Exercise 7

Several consonant blends have *w* as their second letter. They appear at the beginning of words. Note these words: dwarf, swept, twin.

Turn on the skilltape.

Example: $\mathcal{dw}$

1. ____
2. ____
3. ____
4. ____
5. ____

6. ____
7. ____
8. ____
9. ____
10. ____

Record the number of correct answers here and on page 64.

Exercise 7: ____ out of 10 correct

Exercise 8

In this exercise, select a blend from the three given that will form a word when placed in the blank. Then pronounce the word to yourself.

Example: tw, sw, dw $\mathcal{sw}$ill

1. st, tw, dr____amp
2. dr, sw, tw ____in
3. tw, dw, sw ____ell
4. sw, dw, tw ____ice
5. tw, sw, dw ____itch

Note: The blend *tw* in the word "two," or in any word using "two" such as "two-some," will not be pronounced like the *tw* in *tw*ist.

Compare your answers with those given on page 62. Place a checkmark by each of your correct answers. Count the number correct and record that number here and on page 64.

Exercise 8: ____ out of 5 correct

Exercise 9

In this exercise, the words have either a *bl* or *pl* blend. Note the following words: plant, bland.

Turn on the skilltape.

Example: pl

1. *plate*   6. *bleed*
2. *black*   7. *pleet*
3. *blade*   8. *bleet*
4. *player*   9. *plpt*
5. *plied*   10. *blot*

Record the number of correct answers here and on page 64.

Exercise 9: _____ out of 10

Confusing Blends

One set of letters can be confusing because it sometimes looks like a consonant blend but is not. These letters are *sc*. *Sc* is a blend sometimes. *Sc* is a blend when it is immediately followed by the letter *a* (*scat*), by the letter *o* (*score*), or by the letter *u* (*scuff*). Notice that the *sc* in these words makes the sound of *sk*. When *sc* is followed by *e* or *i*, it is not a blend (*scene, scissors*). In such cases, the *sc* has the sound of *s*.

Exercise 10

In this exercise, write *s* if the letters *sc* at the beginning of each word represent a sound like *s*. Write *sk* if the *sc* is a blend.

Example: scaffold *sk*

1. scent _s_   6. scion _s_
2. scoop _sk_   7. sculpture _sk_
3. scuttle _sk_   8. scene _s_
4. scale _sk_   9. scab _sk_
5. science _s_   10. scold _sk_

Compare your answers with those given on page 62. Place a checkmark by each of your correct answers. Count the number correct and record that number here and on page 64.

Exercise 10: ____out of 10 correct

Many times when you hear the *sk* sound, it may be spelled with either *sc* or *sk*, as illustrated in the following words.

sk	*sc*
sky	scat
skin	scalp
ski	scar
sketch	scotch
skull	scout
skunk	scurry
skate	scuba

Turn on Skilltape 3, side B.

Three-letter Blends

Exercise 11

In this exercise, you will name consonant blends which have three letters. Note the blend at the beginning of each of the following words: script, strung, split, spring.

Turn on the skilltape.

Use these three-letter blends in your answers: *scr, str, spl,* and *spr*.

Example: ꙅᴄꭇ

1. ___	6. ___	11. ___	16. ___
2. ___	7. ___	12. ___	17. ___
3. ___	8. ___	13. ___	18. ___
4. ___	9. ___	14. ___	19. ___
5. ___	10. ___	15. ___	20. ___

Record the number of correct answers here and on page 64.

Exercise 11: ____out of 20 correct

Exercise 12

In this exercise, select the appropriate three-letter blend that will form a word when placed in the blank. Then pronounce the word to yourself.

Example: spl, spr _spl_at

1. scr, spr ____een
2. str, spl ____ing
3. str, spr ____eet
4. spr, scr ____ay
5. spl, spr ____ash

6. spr, scr ____eam
7. scr, spl ____int
8. spr, scr ____ing
9. spl, str ____ipe
10. scr, spr ____ap

Compare your answers with those given on page 62. Place a checkmark by each of your correct answers. Count the number correct and record that number here and on page 64.

Exercise 12: ____out of 10 correct

Review Exercise

This exercise will test your ability to blend letters. For each word in the following list, add a consonant to the front of each word to form a blend. Say the first word and then say the new word. There may be more than one new word possible. Write only one.

Example: rag _brag_

1. rash _t/c_
2. rug _d/_
3. lock _b/c_
4. cat _s_
5. mash _s_

6. lack _s/b/c_
7. ring _st/b/sp_
8. kid _s_
9. lamp _c_
10. top _s_

11. rip _t_
12. mug _s_
13. pan _s_
14. nap _l_
15. lad _g_

Now correct your answers using the skilltape.

Turn on the skilltape.

Record the number of correct answers here and on page 64.

Review exercise: ____out of 15 correct

The Ending Blends

Exercise 13

Turn on the skilltape.

Example: 𝒮𝓅

1. ____   6. ____
2. ____   7. ____
3. ____   8. ____
4. ____   9. ____
5. ____   10. ____

Record the number of correct answers here and on page 64.

Exercise 13:   ____out of 10 correct

Exercise 14

In this exercise select an appropriate ending blend that when placed in the blank will form a word. Then pronounce the word to yourself.

Example: -sk, -sp, -st   gho𝓈𝓉

1. -sk, -sp, -st   fea____   6. -sk, -sp, -st   la____
2. -sk, -sp, -st   fa____   7. -sk, -sp, -st   ma____
3. -sk, -sp, -st   a____   8. -sk, -sp, -st   fla____
4. -sk, -sp, -st   cla____   9. -sk, -sp, -st   li____
5. -sk, -sp, -st   bri____   10. -sk, -sp, -st   hu____

Compare your answers with those given on page 62. Place a checkmark by each of your correct answers. Count the number correct and record that number here and on page 64.

Exercise 14:   ____out of 10 correct

Exercise 15

Another group of ending blends which are not used quite so often are *-ft, -ct, -nt, -lt, -ld, -nd, -mp,* and *-pt.* Here are some examples: the *-ft* in *left, -ct* in *fact, -nt* in *tent, -lt* in *belt, -ld* in *cold, -nd* in *band, mp* in *lamp* and *-pt* in *slept.*

For this exercise, select the ending blend that will form a word when you write it in the blank. Then say the word to yourself.

Example: -ld, -mp, -ct   fo*ld*

1. -mp, -nd, -nt   ha_____
2. -nt, -mp, -pt   ju_____
3. -ft, -ct, -pt   le_____
4. -nd, -mp, -ct   fa_____
5. -mp, -ld, -lt   be_____

6. -ld, -pt, -lt   to_____
7. -pt, -ct, -mp   sle_____
8. -mp, -pt, -nt   te_____
9. -lt, -ct, -ld   qui_____
10. -mp, -ct, -ld   we_____

Compare your answers with those given on page 62. Place a checkmark by each of your correct answers. Count the number correct and record that number here and on page 64.

Exercise 15:   _____out of 10 correct

There are some other ending consonant blends which are not used often. These include, *-lf,* as in *elf* and *self; -lp,* as in *help;* and *-lk,* as in *silk.* However, *-lk* and *-lm* usually have a silent *l,* as in *calm, almond, psalm, chalk, talk,* and *walk.* Exceptions to this rule are *elk* and *elm.*

Exercise 16

Turn on the skilltape.

Example: ct   -mp -nd -ft -ct -lt -ld -pt -nt

1. child
2. felt
3. lift
4. spend
5. lamp

6. spient
7. tract
8. left
9. spilt
10. fold

11. champ
12. fund
13. duct
14. hunt
15. tramp

16. swept
17. wilt
18. drift
19. melt
20. mold

Record the number of correct answers here and on page 64.

Exercise 16:   _____out of 20 correct

Posttest A

In this posttest, you will name the blend you hear either at the beginning or end of each word.

Turn on the skilltape.

Example: $\mathcal{CR}$

1. ___	6. ___	11. ___	16. ___	21. ___
2. ___	7. ___	12. ___	17. ___	22. ___
3. ___	8. ___	13. ___	18. ___	23. ___
4. ___	9. ___	14. ___	19. ___	24. ___
5. ___	10. ___	15. ___	20. ___	25. ___

Posttest B

Example: $\mathcal{str}$

1. ___	6. ___
2. ___	7. ___
3. ___	8. ___
4. ___	9. ___
5. ___	10. ___

Posttest C

In this posttest, there are sentences in which a word has been left out. Make a word which contains the blend given in each sentence by filling in the blanks. Be sure the sentence makes sense.

Example: The canary fl*ew* out the door.

1. The cat performed a tr_____ for his master.

2. The woman spl_____ the log into two pieces.

3. The baseball player sc_____ a run.

4. His broken arm had a sl_____ on it.

5. The American flag has thirteen str_____ on it.

6. Tr_____ and bushes are used to decorate parks.

7. The artist dr_____ a picture of the sunset.

8. Claire had a big sm_____ on her face.

9. Fl_____ bloom in May.

10. Larry swept the room with a br_____.

Posttest D

Each of the following sentences has a blend missing from the word. By filling in the blank, make a word which contains one of the ending blends from this list: *-st, -sp, -sk, -ct, -nd, -mp, -pt, -ft, -lt.*

Example: Susan dried the da*mp* wires on the car.

1. The fir____ one in line was the leader.

2. She ke____ a diary in her desk.

3. The soldiers set up ca____ in the woods.

4. People who li____ are said to have a speech problem.

5. His frie____. loaned him the money for the show.

6. The snow will me____ when the sun comes out.

7. The circus clown wore a ma____.

You have now completed the posttests to Chapter 3. Compare your answers to these four posttests with those on page 63 of the worktext. Place a checkmark by each of your correct answers. Count the number correct for each posttest and record your score here and on page 64.

> **Posttest A:**   _____ out of 25 correct
> **Posttest B:**   _____ out of 10 correct
> **Posttest C:**   _____ out of 10 correct
> **Posttest D:**   _____ out of 7 correct
>   **Total:**   _____ out of 52 correct

If you got 47 or more correct, you can go on to the next chapter and take the pretests as directed.

If you got less than 47 correct, talk with your instructor.

Show your instructor the summary sheet on page 64 on which you have recorded your scores for all the exercises and tests.

Answers to Exercises Not on the Skilltape

Exercise 2

1. spice, slice
2. spy, sly, sky, sty
3. steam
4. sting, sling, swing
5. snow, stow, scow, slow

6. small, stall
7. store, snore, spore, score, swore
8. spade
9. snake, stake, slake
10. stare, snare, spare, scare

Exercise 4

1. grand, brand
2. trap, frap
3. bring

4. cringe
5. dream, bream
6. fresh

7. grasp
8. price
9. drop

10. crowd

Exercise 6

1. clock
2. sled, pled
3. plane

4. globe
5. flat, blat
6. play

7. blank
8. clown
9. slide

10. clip

Exercise 8

1. stamp
2. twin

3. dwell, swell

4. twice

5. switch, twitch

Exercise 10

1. s
2. sk
3. sk

4. sk
5. s
6. s

7. sk
8. s
9. sk

10. sk

Exercise 12

1. screen
2. string
3. street

4. spray
5. splash
6. scream

7. splint
8. spring
9. stripe

10. scrap

Exercise 14

1. feast
2. fast
3. ask or asp

4. clasp
5. brisk
6. last

7. mast or mask
8. flask
9. list or lisp

10. husk

Exercise 15

1. hand
2. jump
3. left

4. fact
5. belt
6. told

7. slept
8. tent
9. quilt

10. weld

Answers to Pretests and Posttests

Pretest A

1. br	6. pr	11. gl	16. sp
2. cr	7. tr	12. sl	17. sn
3. dr	8. bl	13. sc (sk)	18. st
4. fr	9. cl	14. sk (sc)	19. sw
5. gr	10. fl	15. sm	20. dw

Pretest B

1. nt	5. sk	9. lf	13. sp
2. mp	6. st	10. ld	14. nt
3. pt	7. ct (kt)	11. nd	15. st
4. nd	8. lt	12. mpt	

Pretest C

1. scr, skr	2. str	3. spl	4. spr

Posttest A

1. bl	8. tr	15. sk	22. pr
2. st	9. nd	16. sc (sk)	23. ld
3. dw	10. sp	17. sm	24. cl (kl)
4. st	11. dr	18. sp	25. fl
5. gl	12. sn	19. sw	
6. st	13. mp	20. ld	
7. tw	14. ct (kt)	21. fr	

Posttest B

1. scr or skr	4. spr	7. spl	10. spl
2. str	5. scr	8. spr	
3. spl	6. str	9. skr or scr	

Posttest C

1. trick	4. sling	7. drew	10. broom
2. split	5. stripes	8. smile, smirk	
3. scored	6. trees	9. flowers	

Posttest D

1. first	3. camp	5. friend	7. mask
2. kept	4. lisp	6. melt	

SUMMARY SHEET

Chapter 3

Record your scores for each test and exercise.

	Number Correct	**Instructor's Comments**
Pretest A	_____out of 20 correct	
Pretest B	_____out of 15 correct	
Pretest C	_____out of 4 correct	
Exercise 1	_____out of 20 correct	
Exercise 2	_____out of 10 correct	
Exercise 3	_____out of 15 correct	
Exercise 4	_____out of 10 correct	
Exercise 5	_____out of 15 correct	
Exercise 6	_____out of 10 correct	
Exercise 7	_____out of 10 correct	
Exercise 8	_____out of 5 correct	
Exercise 9	_____out of 10 correct	
Exercise 10	_____out of 10 correct	
Exercise 11	_____out of 20 correct	
Exercise 12	_____out of 10 correct	
Review Exercise	_____out of 15 correct	
Exercise 13	_____out of 10 correct	
Exercise 14	_____out of 10 correct	
Exercise 15	_____out of 10 correct	
Exercise 16	_____out of 20 correct	
Posttest A	_____out of 25 correct	
Posttest B	_____out of 10 correct	
Posttest C	_____out of 10 correct	
Posttest D	_____out of 7 correct	

4

Beginning and Ending Consonant Digraphs

Glossary

Consonant Digraphs: are two consonants which together represent only one
   sound.
Digraph Blends: three consonants put together that represent two sounds.
Syllables: smaller parts or units of a word containing at least one vowel.

Introduction

Chapter 3 was about consonant blends. This chapter is about other groups of
consonants called *digraphs*. Digraphs, like blends, are consonants that come together at the beginning or end of a word or syllable. However, there is a difference between digraphs and blends. Unlike blends, the pair of consonants in a
digraph stands for only *one* sound, such as the *ch* in *church*, *wh* in *white*, *th* in *think*,
and *sh* in *dish*.

Digraphs may also be put together with one other consonant to form a
digraph blend. Examples of digraph blends are *shr*, as in *shred, thr*, as in *three; chr*,
as in *chrome;* and *sch*, as in *school*.

When you finish this chapter you will be able to spot consonant digraphs
and digraph blends whether they come at the beginning or end of words.

Use Skilltape 4 to help you work through this chapter. The worktext will
tell you when to turn on the skilltape.

The next section is the pretest section for Chapter 4. To see how much of
this chapter you already know, go now to Pretests A, B, and C. Complete each
as well as you can.

Pretest A

Turn on Skilltape 4, side A.

Example: wh

1. ____   6. ____   11. ____   16. ____
2. ____   7. ____   12. ____   17. ____
3. ____   8. ____   13. ____   18. ____
4. ____   9. ____   14. ____   19. ____
5. ____   10. ____   15. ____   20. ____

Pretest B

Example: ng

1. ____   6. ____
2. ____   7. ____
3. ____   8. ____
4. ____   9. ____
5. ____   10. ____

Pretest C

Example: thr

1. ____   6. ____
2. ____   7. ____
3. ____   8. ____
4. ____   9. ____
5. ____   10. ____

Record the number of correct answers here and on page 83.

Pretest A: _____out of 20 correct

Pretest B: _____out of 10 correct

Pretest C: _____out of 10 correct

Total: _____out of 40 correct

If you got 37 or more correct, you may go on to the posttests on pages 78–79.
If you got less than 37 correct, complete this chapter and then take the posttests.

The Digraph PH

Exercise 1

In this exercise, you will learn about the consonant digraph *ph*. The digraph *ph* is pronounced like the letter *f*, as in *phone* and *digraph*.

Turn on the skilltape.

Example: p͟hase

1. photograph	6. phobia
2. graph	7. photo
3. philanthropist	8. phlegm
4. phonics	9. pharmacist
5. physics	10. physical

Record the number of correct answers here and on page 83.

Exercise 1:   _____out of 11 correct

The Digraph SH

Exercise 2

The consonant digraph *sh* is pronounced the way you hear it in these familiar words: *ship* and *dish*.

Turn on the skilltape.

Example: fis͟h

1. wish	6. shelter
2. short	7. thrush
3. sheer	8. crush
4. shoe	9. sheath
5. brash	10. shatter

Record the number of correct answers here and on page 83.

Exercise 2:   _____out of 10 correct

Exercise 3

Turn on the skilltape.

Example: <u>sh</u>

1. ____	6. ____	11. ____	16. ____
2. ____	7. ____	12. ____	17. ____
3. ____	8. ____	13. ____	18. ____
4. ____	9. ____	14. ____	19. ____
5. ____	10. ____	15. ____	20. ____

Record the number of correct answers here and on page 83.

Exercise 3:   ____out of 20 correct

The Digraph CH

Turn on the skilltape.

The consonant digraph *ch* is different from other digraphs because it represents *three* different sounds. In most words, *ch* represents the sound you hear in *child*, *chest*, and *choke*. In some words, the digraph *ch* represents the sound of *k*, as in *chord*, *chorus*, and *chemical*. In still other words, *ch* represents the sound of *sh*, as in *chef*, *chiffon*, *chateau*, and *Chicago*. (Note in your dictionary that most of the words with this last pronunciation come from the French language.)

Exercise 4

Examples: ch as in *chord* <u>k</u>
ch as in *Chicago* <u>sh</u>
ch as in *chest* <u>ch</u>

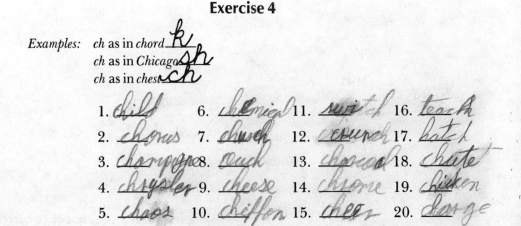

Record the number of correct answers here and on page 83.

Exercise 4: ____out of 20 correct

Exercise 5

As you read the list of words below, pronounce each word to yourself. If you have difficulty recognizing the word, use the examples of the digraph *ch* illustrated below. Write the sound of *ch* you hear in the space provided.

Examples: cheese *ch*
chic *sh*
chorus *k*

1. search *ch*
2. chemistry *k*
3. chore *ch*
4. churn *ch*
5. birch *ch*

6. chef *sh*
7. chime *ch*
8. Christmas *k*
9. pinch *ch*
10. Charlotte *sh*

Compare your answers with those given on page 83. Place a checkmark by each of your correct answers. Count the number correct and record that number here and on page 83.

Exercise 5: ____out of 10 correct

The Digraph TH

The digraph *th* has two sounds. In the word *th*in the *th* is called "unvoiced." In the word *th*is the *th* is "voiced." "Voiced" means that you can feel the vibration in your throat when you say a sound in a word. Try it. Say the word *then*. Is there a vibration when you say the *th*? Yes. The difference between the voiced and unvoiced *th* is the way it is pronounced.

Turn on the skilltape.

Turn on Skilltape 4, side B.

Exercise 6

Example: ___*v*___

1. ___		6. ___	
2. ___		7. ___	
3. ___		8. ___	
4. ___		9. ___	
5. ___		10. ___	

Record the number of correct answers here and on page 83.

Exercise 6:   ___out of 10 correct

Exercise 7

For this list of words, follow these steps:
1. Substitute the digraph *th* for the beginning consonant.
2. Rewrite the word in the space provided.
3. Pronounce the word to yourself.
4. If the *th* is voiced, write a *v* above the word.

Example: bought ___*thought*___

1. hat_____		6. jump_____
2. pen_____		7. pin_____
3. pink_____		8. hem_____
4. ring_____		9. hose_____
5. rank_____		10. dirty_____

Compare your answers with those given on page 81. Place a checkmark by each of your correct answers. Count the number correct and record that number here and on page 83.

Exercise 7:   ___out of 20 correct

Words that have the digraph *th* at the end followed by *e* will be voiced.

Unvoiced	*Voiced*
bath	bathe
breath	breathe
teeth	teethe
cloth	clothe

The Digraph WH

Another consonant digraph is *wh*, as in *wh*at, *wh*eel, *wh*ich, and *wh*y.

Turn on the skilltape.

Exercise 8

Example: t

1. ____   6. ____

2. ____   7. ____

3. ____   8. ____

4. ____   9. ____

5. ____   10. ____

Record the number of correct answers here and on page 84.

Exercise 8: ____out of 10 correct

More About WH

To pronounce the *wh* sound correctly, merely hold the palm of your hand in front of your mouth approximately five inches away. Pretend you are blowing out a candle, and say the word "when." Can you feel the stream of air on your palm? If so, you are pronouncing *wh* correctly.

Exercise 9

In addition to the sound of *wh* that you just heard on the skilltape in Exercise 8, *wh* has another sound found in words such as w̶ho, w̶hole, w̶hom, and w̶hose. In these words, the *w* is silent. In the following list, pronounce each word to yourself, cross out the *w* in the words where *w* is not heard.

Example: whether

1. where	6. whose
2. whole	7. whack
3. why	8. when
4. who	9. whip
5. which	10. whom

Compare your answers with those given on page 81. Place a checkmark by each of your correct answers. Count the number correct and record that number here and on page 83.

Exercise 9:   _____out of 10 correct

Notice that in most words where an *o* follows *wh*, the *w* is silent.

Other Ending Digraphs

Exercise 10

The next digraph to be considered is found only at the end of words. This digraph is *-ng*, as in *wing, sung, king,* and *hang.*

In this exercise, you will find two lists of words. Pronounce each word in the first column to yourself. In column 2, write the word adding *g* at the end. Say the new word.

Example: pan   *pang*

Column 1   Column 2
1. ban   *bang*
2. run
3. son
4. fan
5. sun
6. sin
7. ran
8. kin
9. win
10. bin

Turn on the skilltape.

Record the number of correct answers here and on page 83.

Exercise 10:   _____out of 10 correct

Exercise 11

Another digraph similar to -*ng* is -*nk*. This digraph is also found at the end of words, as in *sink, tank,* and *mink.*

In this exercise, you will find a list of words in the first column. Pronounce each word to yourself. In column 2, write the word adding *k* at the end. Say the new word.

Example: kin   *kink*

Column 1   Column 2
1. sun
2. sin
3. pin
4. ban
5. tan
6. win

Turn on the skilltape.

Record the number of correct answers here and on page 83.

Exercise 11: _____out of 6 correct

The Sound of GH

When the letters *gh* come together, they have three different sounds. *Gh* may sound like *f* as in *tough* or like *g* as in *ghost.* It may also be silent, as in *though.* Table 1 shows the most common words illustrating these sounds.

Table 1

   The Sounds of Gh

gh as f	*gh (silent)*	*gh as g*
rough	weigh	ghost
cough	dough	ghetto
enough	taught	ghoul
tough	high	ghastly
	bought	
	straight	
	fought	
	sigh	

Here are some clues to help you pronounce the letter combination *gh*. If there is an unknown word which contains *gh*, pronounce the word giving *gh* the *f* sound. If you still do not recognize it, pronounce it again without sounding the *gh*.

The Sound of -TCH

Another common combination of consonant letters is *-tch*, as in the word *catch.* This combination of letters sounds exactly like the digraph *ch* in the word *rich*.

The *t* in this combination is silent and is not pronounced. Table 2 lists some of the words which have *-tch*.

Table 2

   Words Ending in -tch

latch	fetch	hitch	notch	clutch
catch	wretch	witch	botch	crutch
scratch	ketch	stitch	crotch	Dutch

Remember when you see the combination *-tch* not to pronounce the *t*. Pronounce the *ch* as in the word *such*.

Digraph Blends

In most textbooks, *sch, chr, shr,* and *thr* are referred to as "blends." However, in each combination there is a digraph that is blended with another consonant. Therefore, we will refer to these three-letter combinations as "digraph blends."

Exercise 12

Turn on the skilltape.

Examples: school *sch* threw *thr* chrome *chr* shrub *shr*

1. ___	6. ___	11. ___
2. ___	7. ___	12. ___
3. ___	8. ___	13. ___
4. ___	9. ___	14. ___
5. ___	10. ___	15. ___

Record the number of correct answers here and on page 83.

Exercise 12: ___out of 15 correct

Exercise 13

In this exercise change the beginning consonant in each word to a digraph blend, using *sch, thr, chr,* or *shr*. Rewrite the word in the blank provided.

Example: tool *school*

1. wink_____
2. lift_____
3. dome_____
4. pool_____
5. rub_____

6. see_____
7. rug_____
8. tone_____
9. sooner_____
10. pill_____

Compare your answers with those given on page 81. Place a checkmark by each of your correct answers. Count the number correct and record that number here and on page 83.

Exercise 13: ___out of 10 correct

Posttest A

The following digraphs may be used in this posttest:
ph (*ph*one), *ch* (*ch*um, *ch*emical, *ch*ef), *sh* (*sh*ut), *th* (*th*en, *th*in), *wh* (*wh*ere)

Turn on the skilltape.

Example: *ph*

1. ____	6. ____	11. ____
2. ____	7. ____	12. ____
3. ____	8. ____	13. ____
4. ____	9. ____	14. ____
5. ____	10. ____	15. ____

Posttest B

Examples: push *sh*   path *th*   pink *nk*   sing *ng*
rich *ch*

1. ____	6. ____
2. ____	7. ____
3. ____	8. ____
4. ____	9. ____
5. ____	10. ____

Posttest C

The following sentences have a word missing. Make a word using one of these digraphs to fit the sentence: ph, ch, sh, th, wh.

Example: The new ___*ship*___ sailed away without taking on water.

1. The ___*phone*___ rang twice before he answered.

2. He ___*chose*___ the young woman for his partner.

3. The man went on a diet and became___*thin*___.
4. The car was waxed and had a beautiful___*shine*___.
5. Bread is a product made from___*wheat*___.

Posttest D

The following sentences have a word missing. Make a word using one of these ending digraphs to complete the sentence: sh, th, nk, ng, ch.

Example: The hunter shot the bird in the___*wing*___.

1. The automobile was wrecked in a two-car___*chrash*___.
2. He was_____by a bee.
3. He had a___*drink*___of water.
4. After she discovered gold, the prospector became
   _____.
5. She was able to hold her___*breath*___under water for a long time.

Posttest E

The following sentences have a word missing. Make a word which contains one of these digraph blends to complete the sentence: shr, chr, thr, sch.

Example: His new jeans___*shrunk*___in the wash.

1. During the___*christmas*___season, department stores are open seven days a week.
2. The thief had a___*scheme*___to steal the jewelry.
3. There are___*three*___bases and a home plate on a base-ball field.
4. The plants and___*shrubs*___around the house made a nice setting.
5. The front and rear bumpers of most cars are made of a metal that looks like___*chrome*___.

Compare your answers to these five posttests with those on page 82. Place a checkmark by each of your correct answers. Count the number correct for each posttest and record your score here and on page 83.

Posttest A: _____out of 15 correct
Posttest B: _____out of 10 correct
Posttest C: _____out of 5 correct
Posttest D: _____out of 5 correct
Posttest E: _____out of 5 correct
Total: _____out of 40 correct

If you got 36 or more correct, you can go on to the next chapter and take the pretests as directed.

If you got less than 36 correct, talk with your instructor.

Show your instructor the summary sheet on page 83 on which you have recorded your scores for all the exercises and tests.

Answers to Exercises Not on the Skilltape

Exercise 5

1. ch	4. ch	7. ch	10. sh
2. k	5. ch	8. k	
3. ch	6. sh	9. ch	

Exercise 7

1. thăt	4. thing	7. thin	10. thirty
2. thĕn	5. thank	8. thĕm	
3. think	6. thump	9. thŏse	

Exercise 9

2. w͎hole	4. w͎ho	6. w͎hose	10. w͎hom

Exercise 13

1. shrink	4. school	7. shrug	10. shrill, thrill
2. thrift, shrift	5. shrub	8. throne	
3. chrome	6. three	9. schooner	

Answers to Pretests and Posttests

Pretest A

1. ph	6. wh	11. shr	16. ph
2. sh	7. th	12. ch	17. wh
3. ch	8. ch	13. chr	18. sh
4. ch or sh	9. th	14. th	19. th
5. ch	10. wh	15. th	20. ph

Pretest B

1. gh	4. th	7. sh	10. ch
2. nk	5. th	8. th	
3. ng	6. ch	9. ng	

Pretest C

1. sch	4. thr	7. shr	10. thr
2. chr	5. chr	8. chr	
3. shr	6. sch	9. shr	

Posttest A

1. ch	5. ch	9. ch	13. sh
2. wh	6. ph	10. sh	14. th
3. th	7. sh	11. ch	15. ph
4. th	8. th	12. th	

Posttest B

1. sh	4. ng	7. th	10. ch
2. th	5. ch	8. nk	
3. nk	6. sh	9. ng	

Posttest C

1. phone	3. thin	4. shine	5. wheat
2. chose			

Posttest D

1. crash	3. drink or	4. rich	5. breath
2. stung	dish or		
	tank		

Posttest E

1. Christmas	3. three	4. shrubs or	5. chrome
2. scheme		shrubbery	

SUMMARY SHEET

Chapter 4

Record your scores for each test and exercise.

	Number Correct	**Instructor's Comments**
Pretest A	_____out of 20 correct	
Pretest B	_____out of 10 correct	
Pretest C	_____out of 10 correct	
Exercise 1	_____out of 11 correct	
Exercise 2	_____out of 10 correct	
Exercise 3	_____out of 20 correct	
Exercise 4	_____out of 20 correct	
Exercise 5	_____out of 10 correct	
Exercise 6	_____out of 10 correct	
Exercise 7	_____out of 20 correct	
Exercise 8	_____out of 10 correct	
Exercise 9	_____out of 10 correct	
Exercise 10	_____out of 10 correct	
Exercise 11	_____out of 6 correct	
Exercise 12	_____out of 15 correct	
Exercise 13	_____out of 10 correct	
Posttest A	_____out of 15 correct	
Posttest B	_____out of 10 correct	
Posttest C	_____out of 5 correct	
Posttest D	_____out of 5 correct	
Posttest E	_____out of 5 correct	

5

Long Vowels

Glossary

Vowels: these letters in the alphabet — *a, e, i, o, u,* and sometimes *w* and *y*.
Long Vowels: vowels that are sounded the way they are said in reciting the alphabet.

Introduction

The vowels are *a, e, i, o, u* and sometimes *w* or *y*. All words must have a vowel. Each vowel represents at least two sounds. This chapter will deal with the *long* sound of vowels. Other vowel sounds will be covered in Chapters 6 and 7.

When you finish this chapter, you will be able to hear the difference between long vowel sounds and other vowel sounds. You will also be able to know what conditions make vowels long. With this knowledge, you will be able to pronounce words which contain long vowel sounds.

Use Skilltape 5 to help you work through this chapter. The directions in this worktext will tell you when to turn on the skilltape.

The next section contains the pretests for Chapter 5. To see how much of the material in this chapter you already know, go now to Pretests A and B. Complete each one the best you can.

Pretest A

In the following sentences, select the word in parentheses which contains the long vowel sound.

Example: The   teacher   ___*wrote*___ the   question   on   the   blackboard.   (wrote, scrawled)

1. For my son's fourth birthday, I bought the __*cake*__ for the party.   (cake, punch)

2. To help them wake up in the morning, people wash their __*face*__ (face, hands)

3. In planting the garden, a __*tree*__ was planted near the house.   (tree, bush)

4. One of my favorite vegetables is __*peas*__.   (peas, carrots)

5. In the third inning of the game, the outfielder made a good __*throw*__.   (catch, throw)

✗ 6. The students walked __*past*__ the cafeteria on the way to their next class.   (past, (by))

7. Since the __*play*__ was a good one, the audience applauded loudly.   (play, band)

Pretest B

Turn on Skilltape 5, side A.

Example: *a*

✓1. *a*	✓6. *u*	✓11. *u*	✓16. *i*
2. *e*	7. *a*	✓12. *e*	17. *e*
✓3. *a*	8. *u*	✓13. *a*	✗18. *e* (u)
4. *a*	9. *e*	✓14. *o*	19. *a*
✓5. *e*	✓10. *i*	15. *u*	20. *i*

Record the number of correct answers here and on page 108.

Pretest A: __6__ out of 7 correct
Pretest B: __9__ out of 20 correct
Total: __15__ out of 27 correct

If you got 24 or more correct, you may go on to the posttests on pages 104–105.
If you got less than 24 correct, complete this chapter and then take the posttests.

Vowels in the Alphabet

What letter would you put in the blank to make these letters a word?

c___t

If you inserted an *a, o,* or *u,* you would make one of these words: *cat, cot,* or *cut.*
What are the letters *a, o,* and *u* called? ___*long vowels*___ If you wrote "vowels,"
you would be right. All words must have at least one vowel. You learned in an
earlier chapter that the alphabet consists of 26 letters called consonants and
vowels. Of the 26 letters, 5 are vowels. These vowels are *a, e, i, o,* and *u,* and
sometimes *w* and *y.*

This chapter deals with the long sound of these vowels.

> *Long vowels* are vowels
> that are sounded the
> way they are said in the
> alphabet.

Turn on the skilltape.

Sound of Long A

Exercise 1

In this exercise, you will listen to 20 words which contain the letter *a.* If the word contains a long vowel sound, mark an *L.* If it has a different sound, leave it blank.

Turn on the skilltape.

Example: _ℓ_

1. _ℓ_   5. _ℓ_   9. _ℓ_   13. _ℓ_   17. _ℓ_
2. _ℓ_   6. _ℓ_   10. _ℓ_   14. _ℓ_   18. _ℓ_
3. _ℓ_   7. ___   11. _ℓ_   15. _ℓ_   19. _ℓ_
4. _ℓ_   8. ___   12. _ℓ_   16. _ℓ_   20. _ℓ_

Record the number of correct answers here and on page 108.

Exercise 1: ___ **out of 20 correct**

Exercise 2

Say each of the following words to yourself. Then select the one word in each line which has the long sound of *a*. Write that word in the blank space at the right. Say the word. Can you hear the long vowel sound of *a*?

Example: claw, grate, plank, tab ___*grate*___

1. cake, far, bag, awful___*cake*___
2. ash, plane, father, sand___*plane*___
3. hand, fall, plant, late___*late*___
4. harp, brand, flat, safe___*safe*___
5. law, stake, land, sad___*stake*___

Turn on the skilltape.

Record the number of correct answers here and on page 108.

Exercise 2:   _5_ out of 5 correct

Rules for Recognizing Long A

Although there are exceptions, there are some general rules which can help you in recognizing long *a* vowels.

Rule 1: When there are two vowels in a word, one of which is final *e*, the first vowel is often long and the final e is silent. For example: *fake, cage, lame, sale.*

Rule 2: If *a* and *y* are together, this combination makes the long sound of *a*. For example: *say, play, tray, gray, pray, clay.*

Rule 3: When *ai* comes at the beginning of a word, it has the long sound of *a*, as in *aid, ail, aim.* Sometimes *ai* has the long vowel sound in the middle of a word, as in *fail, braid, tail, paint, bait.* However, there are some exceptions, such as *said* and *plaid.*

Exercise 3

Here is a list of words, some of which have long *a* sounds. Underline those words which have that sound.

Example: ✓crate

✓1. tame	✗6. said	✓11. lack	✓16. plaid
✓2. gate	✓7. tray	✓12. game	✓17. match
✓3. lamb	✓8. lash	✓13. stay	✗18. ache
✓4. plant	✓9. brass	✓14. braid	✓19. bad
✓5. paint	✓10. cake	✓15. bake	✓20. stage

Turn on the skilltape.

Record the number of correct answers here and on page 108.

Exercise 3: ___18___ **out of 20 correct**

Exercise 4

In the following list of words, there are some with long *a* sounds and some without long *a* sounds. Complete the sentences with a word that contains the long *a* sound.

hat	grapes	snacks	made
tag	bag	bake	grabbed
stand	cape	hay	wrapped

Example: Don't ___bake___ the cookie dough until later.

✓1. She tried on a new ___cape___.

✓2. At the market he bought ___grapes___ for the children.

✓3. The young children liked to play in the ___hay___.

✓4. Mother ___made___ a gift for the party.

Turn on the skilltape.

Record the number of correct answers here and on page 108.

Exercise 4: ___4___ **out of 4 correct**

Sound of Long E

Look at these words: eat, Pete, sleep, team, piece. Say each word to yourself. What vowel sound do you hear in these words? You should hear the long sound of *e*.

Exercise 5

In this exercise, you will listen to 20 words which contain the letter *e*. If the word contains a long vowel sound, mark an L in the space provided. If the word has a different vowel sound, leave the space empty.

Turn on the skilltape.

Example: _ℓ_

1. _ℓ_   5. _ℓ_   9. _ℓ_   13. _ℓ_   17. ____
2. ____ 6. _ℓ_   10. ____ 14. ____ 18. _ℓ_
3. _ℓ_   7. _ℓ_   11. _ℓ_   15. ____ 19. _ℓ_
4. ____ 8. _ℓ_   12. _ℓ_   16. _ℓ_   20. _ℓ_

Record the number of correct answers here and on page 108.

Exercise 5:   _17_ out of 20 correct

Exercise 6

Say each of the following words to yourself. Then select the word in the line which has the long sound of *e*. Write that word in the blank at the right. Say the word. Can you hear the long sound of *e*?

Example: Sell, pen, greet, west___*greet*___

1. peek, bed, melt, perk___*peek*___
2. leg, her, knee, them___*knee*___
3. me, felt, hen, desk___*me*___
4. each, bed, blend, crest___*each*___
5. twelve, sheep, letter, get___*sheep*___

Turn on the skilltape.

Record the number of correct answers here and on page 108.

Exercise 6:   _5_ out of 5 correct

Rules for Recognizing Long E

The sound of long *e* can be recognized in several ways.

> *Rule 1:* When there are two *e*'s together in a word, the vowel sound is generally long *e*. For example: *feet, tree, sheet, free.*

> *Rule 2:* When the vowel *e* comes at the end of a word and it is the *only* vowel, the *e* is generally long. For example: *we, she, he, be, me.*

There are several other combinations of vowels which make the long sound of *e*. These vowels will be discussed in Chapter 7, called "Varying Vowels." However, there is one combination of vowels which could be discussed here. When the letters *ea* come together, the vowel sound is often that of long *e*. For example: *steam, beam, real, steal, meat.* This rule is not as safe as the two rules stated earlier, because there are many exceptions. For example: *bread, thread, spread, steak, break.*

Exercise 7

Here is a list of words, some of which have the long *e* sound. Underline those words which have that sound.

Example: <u>teak</u>

1. herd	6. chest	11. creep	16. break
2. pet	7. men	12. step	17. sheen
3. left	8. steep	13. she	18. free
4. set	9. mean	14. three	19. bed
5. sheet	10. steed	15. deck	20. then

Turn on the skilltape.

Record the number of correct answers here and on page 108.

Exercise 7: __18__ **out of 20 correct**

Exercise 8

In the following list, there are some words which contain the long *e* sound. Complete the sentences below using words from the list with long *e* sounds.

beef	sheep	jello
bet	elms	legs
feet	beets	pet

Example: _____*Beef*_____cattle are grown on ranches.

✓ 1. The runner's_____*feet*_____were sore.

✓ 2. They had_____*beef*_____for lunch.

✓ 3. He took the_____*sheep*_____to the veterinarian.

✓ 4. The family planted_____*beets*_____in the backyard.

Turn on the skilltape.

Record the number of correct answers here and on page 108.

Exercise 8:   _4_out of 4 correct

Sound of Long I

Look at these words: *pine, smile, try, right, mind.* Say each word to yourself. What vowel sound do you hear in these words? You should hear the long sound of *i.*

Exercise 9

In this exercise, you will listen to 20 words which contain the letter *i.* If the word contains a long vowel sound of *i,* mark an L (for long) in the space provided. If it has a different sound, leave the space empty.

Turn on the skilltape.

Example: *L*

✓1. ___	✓5. *l*	✓9. ___	✓13. *l*	✓17. ___
✓2. *l*	✓6. ___	✓10. ___	✓14. ___	✓18. *l*
✓3. ___	✓7. *l*	✓11. ___	✓15. *l*	✓19. *l*
✓4. ___	✓8. *l*	✓12. ___	✓16. *l*	✓20. *l*

Record the number of correct answers here and on page 108.

Exercise 9:   _20_out of 20 correct

Exercise 10

Say each word to yourself. Then select the word in the line which has the long sound of *i*. Write that word in the blank space. Say the word. Can you hear the long sound of *i*?

Example: climb, jib, grip, glib ___*climb*___

1. mile, pill, give, bird___*mile*___
2. bill, whip, third, line___*line*___
3. fly, pin, brick, chip___*fly*___
4. lit, light, dirt, fix___*light*___
5. city, sin, kind, spin___*kind*___

Turn on the skilltape.

Record the number of correct answers here and on page 108.

Exercise 10:   _5_ out of 5 correct

Rules for Recognizing Long I

Although there are some exceptions to the rules, there are some general rules which can be helpful in recognizing long *i* vowels.

Rule 1:   When there are two vowels in a word, one of which is a final *e*, the first vowel is often long and the final *e* is silent. For example: *pine, slide, dime, bribe*.

Rule 2:   When the vowel *i* is followed by *-ld* or *-nd*, the *i* is frequently long. For example: *wild, child, mild, mind, kind, find, bind*.

Rule 3:   The vowel *i* followed by *gh* has a long sound and the *gh* is silent. For example: *tight, might, sight*.

Rule 4:   When the letter *y* comes at the end of a small word, it has the sound of long *i*. For example: *dry, try, fly, my, by, shy*. (There will be more about the letter "y" in Chapter 8.)

Turn on Skilltape 5, side B.

Exercise 11

Underline those words in the following list which have the sound of long *i*.

Example: glide

1. rip	5. fright	9. grim	13. pride	17. crime
2. thigh	6. slip	10. skin	14. hip	18. sigh
3. trip	7. hide	11. dirt	15. ripe	19. dry
4. slide	8. by	12. brine	16. shift	20. file

Turn on the skilltape.

Record the number of correct answers here and on page 108.

Exercise 11:   *20* **out of 20 correct**

Exercise 12

Select words from the following list which have the long *i* sound and use one for each of the following sentences.

hide	flight	skin	sit
thin	trip	fine	thigh

Example: Lisa prefers the *thigh* to the drumstick when she eats fried chicken.

1. Do not *hide* behind the couch.
2. She bruised her *thigh* when she fell off the bike.
3. The *flight* to California was a fast one.
4. He was a *fine* runner.

Turn on the skilltape.

Record the number of correct answers here and on page 108.

Exercise 12:   *4* **out of 4 correct**

Sound of Long O

Look at these words: *note, float, cold, goes, blow, tow.* Say each word to yourself. What vowel sound do you hear in these words? You should hear the long sound of *o.*

Exercise 13

In this exercise, you will listen to 20 words which contain the letter *o.* If the word contains the long sound of the letter, mark an L (for long) in the space provided. If it has a sound different than the long sound, leave it blank.

Turn on the skilltape.

Example: _L_

1. ___	5. ___	9. ___	13. ___	17. ___
2. ___	6. ___	10. ___	14. ___	18. ___
3. ___	7. ___	11. ___	15. ___	19. ___
4. ___	8. ___	12. ___	16. ___	20. ___

Record the number of correct answers here and on page 108.

Exercise 13:   ___out of 20 correct

Exercise 14

In this exercise, say each word to yourself. Then select the word in the line which has the long sound of *o.* Write that word in the blank space at the right. Say the word.

Example: plot, cone, tot, crotch___*cone*___

   1. stop, bone, lost, port___*port*___

   2. snow, dog, trot, box___*snow*___

   3. rock, goat, logs, top___*goat*___

   4. rot, sports, cold, lock___*sport*___

Turn on the skilltape.

Record the number of correct answers here and on page 108.

Exercise 14:   _4_out of 4 correct

Rules for Recognizing Long O

Turn on the skilltape.

Although there are exceptions to these rules, there are some general rules which can be helpful in recognizing long *o* vowels.

Rule 1:   When there are two vowels in a word, one of which is final *e*, the first vowel is long and the final *e* is silent. For example: *pose, tone, hope, stone.*

Rule 2:   In many cases when the vowels *o* and *a* come together, the long sound of *o* is heard. For example: *toast, boast, boat, load, toad, soap.*

Rule 3:   When the letter *o* is followed by the consonant *l*, often the *o* is long. For example: *roll, cold, bold, sold, colt, bolt.*

Rule 4:   When the letter *o* is followed by the letter *w*, it has the sound of long *o* about half the time. (The other sound which *ow* makes will be discussed in Chapter 7.) Some examples of the long sound of *ow* are *snow, flow, crow, row, grow, slow, glow, own, mow, tow.*

Exercise 15

Here is a list of words, some of which have the long *o* sound. Underline those words which have that sound. Say each word to yourself.

Example: mold

1. goat	5. bolt	9. horse	13. got	17. those
2. hot	6. stone	10. cow	14. shot	18. flow
3. loom	7. bold	11. soap	15. short	19. bone
4. load	8. fog	12. flop	16. blow	20. stop

Turn on the skilltape.

Record the number of correct answers here and on page 108.

Exercise 15:   ___19___ out of 20 correct

Exercise 16

Select words from the following list which have the long *o* sound to complete the sentences below

boat	colt	stones	cow
goat	horse	rocks	sloop

Example: The New England countryside was filled with ___*stones*___ that made farming difficult.

1. The ___*boat*___ was tied up at the pier.
2. The farmer was milking the ___*goat*___.
3. David put the ___*stones*___ in his sling to kill the giant.
4. Running in the pasture was the beautiful gray ___*colt*___.

Turn on the skilltape.

Record the number of correct answers here and on page 108.

Exercise 16:   ___4___ **out of 4 correct**

Sound of Long U

Look at these words: *mute, mule, cute, muse, cube.* Say each word to yourself. What vowel sound do you hear in these words? You should hear the long sound of *u.*

Look at these words: *tune, duke, tube, dune.* The *u* in these words represents the sound of either long *u* as in *fume,* or *oo* as in *boot.*

Exercise 17

In this exercise, you will listen to 20 words which contain the letter *u.* If a word contains the long vowel sound of *u* or the sound of *oo* as in *boot,* mark an L (for long) in the space provided. If it has a different vowel sound, leave it blank.

Turn on the skilltape.

Example: *L*

1. ___	3. ___	5. ___	7. ___	9. ___
2. ___	4. ___	6. ___	8. ___	10. ___

11. ____	13. ____	15. ____	17. ____	19. ____
12. ____	14. ____	16. ____	18. ____	20. ____

Record the number of correct answers here and on page 108.

Exercise 17:   ____ out of 20 correct

Exercise 18

Say each word to yourself. Determine whether you can hear the long sound of *u*. Write the word which has the long sound of *u* in the blank at the right. Then say the word again. Can you hear the long sound of *u*?

Example: put, cluck, cut, mute _*mute*_

  1. duck, fun, fur, use _*use*_
  2. cute, brush, bunk, lunch _*cute*_
  3. truck, duke, thump, stung _*duke*_
  4. crumb, hung, huge, lump _*huge*_
  5. cuke, mud, hush, stunt _*cuke*_

Compare your answers with those given on page 106. Place a checkmark by each of your correct answers. Count the number correct and record that number here and on page 108.

Exercise 18:   _5_ out of 5 correct

Rules for Recognizing Long U

Although there are exceptions, there are some general rules which can be helpful in recognizing long *u* vowels.

Rule 1:   When there are two vowels in a word, one of which is final *e,* the first vowel is usually long and the final *e* is silent. For example: *huge, cute, use, cube.* For words like *duke, tube,* and *June,* different areas of the country may pronounce them as *dook, toob, Joon.*
      Another major exception to rule one is in words such as *rule, crude, prune, rude, flute, brute.* Even though these words seem to

follow the above rule, they do not. *It is impossible to make the* u *sound long in any word which has an* r *before the* u. And it is almost impossible to make a long sound of *u* when an *l* comes before the *u*.

Rule 2: In some words the letter combinations *ue* and *ew* have the sound of long *u*. For example: *few, fuel, cue, pew,* However, in many words *ew* and *ue* have the vowel sound you hear in the word *boot*. This is due to dialect and to the impossible letter combinations that occur when *l* and *r* are placed before *ew* or *ue*. For example: *brew, clue, threw, blue, true, glue*.

Rule 3: It is safe to say that the long sound of *u* may be sounded as a long u, y$\overline{oo}$ as in *cute* and *fuel*, and it may be sounded $\overline{oo}$, as *brute* and *true* (rhyming with b**oo**t).

Exercise 19

Underline those words in the following list which have the long sound of *u* — either y$\overline{oo}$ or $\overline{oo}$.

Example: <u>truth</u>

1. <u>cue</u>	5. <u>brute</u>	9. <u>stew</u>	13. flush	17. brunt
2. dump	6. dust	10. <u>duke</u>	14. trunk	18. crust
✗ 3. <u>dunes</u>	7. <u>blue</u>	11. <u>mule</u>	15. <u>mute</u>	19. <u>rule</u>
4. <u>cute</u>	8. <u>few</u>	12. <u>skew</u>	16. stung	20. <u>threw</u>

Compare your answers with those given on page 106. Place a checkmark by each of your correct answers. Count the number correct and record that number here and on page 108.

Exercise 19: _19_ **out of 20 correct**

Exercise 20

Below is a list of 20 words. Some of them have the sound of the long vowel *u* (y$\overline{oo}$). Some have the same sound you hear in the word boot $\overline{oo}$. Some of the words may be pronounced either way. In the chart below, write the words from the list in the appropriate column, depending on how you hear the vowel sound. The example word *lute* has been done for you.

huge	true	cube	tube	cue
fuse	few	rule	chew	tune
duke	rude	prune	pew	flue
flute	fume	stew	brew	crew

u ($y\overline{oo}$) (as in *use*)	u($\overline{oo}$) (as in *boot*)	either u ($y\overline{oo}$) or u($\overline{oo}$)
huge *fuse* *fume* *cue* *few* *cube* *pew*	*lute* *true* *chew* *brew* *flute* *flue* *rude* *rule* *crew* *prune*	*tube* *stew* *tune* *duke*

Compare your answers with those given on page 106. Place a checkmark by each of your correct answers. Count the number correct and record them here and on page 108.

Exercise 20: __14__out of 20 correct

Review Exercise A

There are three words in each line of this exercise. Some are nonsense words and some are real words. On the skilltape, you will hear one word read from each line. Underline the word read on the skilltape.

Turn on the skilltape.

1. chayst   shayt ✓   chaisk ✓
2. drize   ✓brise   dris
3.✓ threed   ✓reed   ✓dreeth
4. wheanch   whench   ✓wheensh
5. doze ✓   thoze   throde ✓

6. blaik ✓	✓plaik	flaik ✓
7. drone	drown ✓	brone ✓
8. swade ✓	swad	sweed
9. briske ✓	brist	briste
10. scupe	clake ✓	scup
11. smade ✓	spreed ✓	scrade ✓
12. preste	preske ✓	breste
13. cligh	klee ✓	squeed ✓
14. dwoap	dwop	dwup
15. splay ✓	stray ✓	spray ✓
16. scrate ✓	skate ✓	state ✓
17. freetch ✓	preesh ✓	freest ✓
18. twoast ✓	troste	throap
19. flait ✓	wait ✓	quait ✓
20. sleen ✓	kleen	keen ✓

Record the number of correct answers here and on page 108.

Review Exercise A: _20_ out of 20 correct

Review Exercise B

All the words in this exercise are nonsense words. Select the word in each line which has a long vowel sound. Remember your clues for recognizing long vowels. Say each word to yourself first. Then underline the word which has the long vowel sound.

1. brate	sprat	trad
2. fum	stume	strunk
3. sprot	spoat	thort
4. spright	thritch	brinsh
5. chesh	screegh	wheth
6. cread	gred	brend
7. stile	stim	strim

8. sprin	sline	stip
9. bost	bolp	brom
10. strind	shint	tris
11. stromp	stotch	strow
12. thron	throbe	throd
13. bew	schoom	brue
14. whate	whart	thamk
15. fong	froanth	sloph
16. phine	mingh	slif
17. jom	jold	job
18. threeph	hench	flemp
19. hulth	bule	hurds
20. glank	traypt	stet

Compare your answers with those given on page 106. Place a checkmark by each of your correct answers. Count the number correct and record that number here and on page 108.

Review Exercise B: ___18___ out of 20 correct

Review Exercise C

In this exercise, write 1 in the space if the first word read on the tape has the long vowel sound. Write 2 if the second word has the long vowel sound.

Turn on the skilltape.

Example: ___2___

1. ___	5. ___	9. ___	13. ___	17. ___
2. ___	6. ___	10. ___	14. ___	18. ___
3. ___	7. ___	11. ___	15. ___	19. ___
4. ___	8. ___	12. ___	16. ___	20. ___

Record the number of correct answers here and on page 108.

Review Exercise C: ___ out of 20 correct

P
O
S
T
E
S
T
S

Posttest A

In the following sentences, select that word in parentheses that contains a long vowel and completes the sentence.

Example: I'll be staying out until ___*nine*___ o'clock tonight. (nine, ten)

1. She was going on a ___*date*___ this Saturday.   (date, trip)

2. The dog jumped over the ___*gate*___.   (gate, fence)

3. He began to ___*peel*___ the apple.   (peel, cut

4. The man received his ___*pay*___ last week.   (check, pay)

5. When they entered the house, they switched on a ___*light*___.   (lamp, light)

6. For dinner she was planning to cook ___*cube*___ steaks.   (rib, cube)

7. The carpet had a ___*stain*___ on it from the spilled drink.   (spot, stain)

8. He was so broke, he didn't have a ___*dime*___.   (dime, cent)

9. They painted the ___*dome*___ of the capitol building.   (top, dome)

10. She planned to take a trip on a ___*boat*___.   (ship, boat)

Posttest B

In the following list of nonsense words, underline those words that have a long vowel sound. Remember the clues for recognizing long vowels. Say each word to yourself.

Example: plox (no underline)

1. cre	5. trine	9. trone	13. fube	17. bry
2. berz	6. pesh	10. purn	14. fane	18. tus
3. chay	7. sait	11. fild	15. stread	19. stright
4. lar	8. crit	12. shoam	16. breen	20. flom

Posttest C

Turn on the skilltape.

Example: $\underline{O}$

1. _a_	5. ___	9. _a_	13. _o_	17. ___
2. _e_	6. _o_	10. _i_	14. ___	18. ___
3. ___	7. _u_	11. ___	15. ___	19. ___
4. _i_	8. ___	12. _e_	16. _i_	20. ___

Record the number of correct answers here and on page 108.

Posttest A: _10_ **out of 10 correct**
Posttest B: _18_ **out of 20 correct**
Posttest C: _20_ **out of 20 correct**
Total: _48_ **out of 50 correct**

If you got 45 or more correct, you can go on to the next chapter and take the pretests as directed.

If you got less than 45 correct, talk with your instructor.

Show your instructor the summary sheet on page 108 on which you have recorded your scores for all the exercises and tests.

Answers to Exercises Not on the Skilltape

Exercise 18

1. use   2. cute   3. duke   4. huge   5. cuke

Exercise 19

Underline these numbers: 1, 3*, 4, 5, 7, 8, 9*, 10*, 11, 12, 15, 19, 20

*These words may be pronounced either way.

Exercise 20

u (yo͞o) (as in use)	u (o͞o) (as in boot)	u (yo͞o) or u (o͞o)
huge	flute	tube
fuse	true	tune
few	rude	stew
fume	rule	duke
cube	prune	
cue	chew	
pew	brew	
	blue	
	crew	

Review Exercise A

1. chayst	5. thoze	9. briske	13. cligh	17. freest
2. drize	6. plaik	10. scupe	14. dwoap	18. troste
3. threed	7. drone	11. scrade	15. splay	19. flait
4. wheanch	8. sweed	12. preske	16. scrate	20. keen

Review Exercise B

1. brate	5. screegh	9. bolp	13. bew	17. jold
2. stume	6. cread	10. strind	14. whate	18. threeph
3. spoat	7. stile	11. strow	15. froanth	19. bule
4. spright	8. sline	12. throbe	16. phine	20. traypt

Answers to Pretests and Posttests

Pretest A

1. cake	3. tree	5. throw	7. play
2. face	4. peas	6. by	

Pretest B

1. o	6. u	13. a	18. u
3. a	10. i	14. o	
5. e	12. e	16. i	

Posttest A

1. date	4. pay	7. stain	10. boat
2. gate	5. light	8. dime	
3. peel	6. cube	9. dome	

Posttest B

1. cre	7. sait	13. fube	16. breen
3. chay	9. trone	14. fane	17. bry
5. trine	12. shoam	15. stread	19. stright

Posttest C

1. a	6. o	10. i	16. i
2. e	7. u	12. e	
4. i	9. a	13. o	

SUMMARY SHEET

Chapter 5

Record your scores for each test and exercise.

	Number Correct	**Instructor's Comments**
Pretest A	____out of 7 correct	
Pretest B	____out of 20 correct	
Exercise 1	____out of 20 correct	
Exercise 2	____out of 5 correct	
Exercise 3	____out of 20 correct	
Exercise 4	____out of 4 correct	
Exercise 5	____out of 20 correct	
Exercise 6	____out of 5 correct	
Exercise 7	____out of 20 correct	
Exercise 8	____out of 4 correct	
Exercise 9	____out of 20 correct	
Exercise 10	____out of 5 correct	
Exercise 11	____out of 20 correct	
Exercise 12	____out of 4 correct	
Exercise 13	____out of 20 correct	
Exercise 14	____out of 4 correct	
Exercise 15	____out of 20 correct	
Exercise 16	____out of 4 correct	
Exercise 17	____out of 20 correct	
Exercise 18	____out of 5 correct	
Exercise 19	____out of 20 correct	
Exercise 20	____out of 20 correct	
Review Exercise A	____out of 20 correct	
Review Exercise B	____out of 20 correct	
Review Exercise C	____out of 20 correct	
Posttest A	____out of 10 correct	
Posttest B	____out of 20 correct	
Posttest C	____out of 20 correct	

6

Short Vowels

Glossary

Short Vowels: vowels that represent the sound of *a* as in *hat, e* as in *bet, i* as in
    bit, o as in *hot,* and *u* as in *but.*

Introduction

Chapter 5 covered the long vowel sounds. This chapter will deal with the short vowel sounds. You may recall that when a long vowel is pronounced in a word, it sounds the same way it does when the letter is said as you recite the alphabet. The short vowel sounds are different, because they do not sound like their letter names. This chapter will enable you to pick out and say short vowel sounds in words. You will also be able to see and hear the difference between a short vowel sound and other vowel sounds. As a result, you will be able to sound out words containing short vowels.

Use Skilltape 6 to help you work through this chapter. The directions in this worktext will tell you when to turn on the skilltape.

The next section contains the pretests for Chapter 6. To see how much of the material in this chapter you already know, go now to Pretests A and B. Complete each to the best of your ability.

110

Pretest A

Turn on Skilltape 6, side A.

Example: _l_

1. ____	5. ____	9. ____	13. ____	17. ____
2. ____	6. ____	10. ____	14. ____	18. ____
3. ____	7. ____	11. ____	15. ____	19. ____
4. ____	8. ____	12. ____	16. ____	20. ____

Pretest B

In the following sentences, select that word in parentheses that contains a short vowel sound.

Example: The _candle_ stopped   burning   only   after   we   fell asleep.   (candle, fire)

1. We took a ride in a_____.   (car, cab, train)

2. The gentleman went into a store and bought a new _____.   (coat, hat)

3. A popular summer fruit is a_____.   (plum, peach)

4. The girls and boys at summer camp like to _____during their spare time.   (swim, hike)

5. David threw a_____at Goliath.   (rock, stone)

6. There were_____girls playing ball in the field. (three, ten)

Compare your answers to these pretests with those on page 132. Place a checkmark by each of your correct answers. Count the number correct for each pretest and write that number in the space provided here and on page 133.

Pretest A: _____out of 20 correct
Pretest B: _____out of 6 correct
Total: _____out of 26 correct

If you got 23 or more correct, you may go on to the posttests on pages 128–29.
If you got less than 23 correct, complete this chapter and then take the posttests.

Sound of Short A

Exercise 1

Look at the following two lists of words. The first column contains words that have the long *a* sound. The second column contains words that have the short *a* sound.

Turn on the skilltape.

Long	Short
made	mad
hate	hat
rate	rat
mate	mat
fate	fat

Example: ___L___

1. __S__ *pal*
2. __L__ *rate*
3. __S__ *man*
4. __S__ *fat*
5. __L__ *fade*

6. __L__ *main*
7. __L__ *pale*
8. __S__ *pan*
9. __S__ *fad*
10. __L__ *pain*

Record the number of correct answers here and on page 133

Exercise 1:   _____out of 10 correct

Exercise 2

In this exercise, say each word in each line to yourself. Select the word in each line that has the short sound of *a*. Write that word in the blank at the right. Say the word again. Can you hear the short vowel sound of *a* as in *at*?

Example: place, rail, track, faint *track*

1. cake, tar, lack, call *lack*
2. flap, rate, tear, ball *flap*
3. band, stare, halt, bait *band*
4. say, black, trace, law *black*
5. slat, day, stain, tall *slat*

Compare your answers with those given on page 130. Place a checkmark by each of your correct answers. Count the number correct and record that number here and on page 133.

Exercise 2:   _____out of 5 correct

General Rule for Short A

There is one general rule that can be helpful in recognizing short vowels. A vowel is usually short when it is the only vowel in the word and is immediately followed by a consonant. Examples: *at, bat, stag, shack.*

However, there are some exceptions, as in *call, ball, car,* and *bar.* In these words, the sound of *a* is changed because of the *l* and *r.* These sounds will be discussed in Chapter 7.

Exercise 3

Using the information you have just learned, complete the following exercise. In the following list of words, there are some with short *a* sounds, some with long *a* sounds, and some that have neither. Complete each of the following sentences with a word from the list that has the short *a* sound.

camp	face	bass	shank
race	gray	stage	pail
hands	black	pan	bake

Example: The ___*black*___ car skidded to a stop.

1. My friends decided to go to a ___*camp*___ this summer.

2. Did you wash your ___*hands*___ today?

3. The new jacket had a ___*black*___ collar.

4. He caught a huge ___*bass*___ on the fishing trip.

5. There was a leak in the roof. He put a ___*pan*___ under it to catch the water.

Compare your answers with those given on page 130. Place a checkmark by each of your correct answers. Count the number correct and record that number here and on page 133.

Exercise 3:   _____out of 5 correct

Sound of Short E

Exercise 4

Look at the following lists of words. The first column contains words that have the long
e sound. The second column contains words that have the short *e* sound.

Turn on the skilltape.

Long	Short
she	shed
beat	bet
breed	bred
scene	shred
these	then

Example:

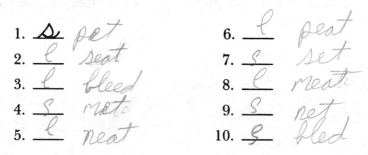

1. *L* pet
2. *l* seat
3. *l* bleed
4. *S* mate
5. *l* neat

6. *l* peat
7. *S* set
8. *l* meat
9. *S* net
10. *S* bled

Record the number of correct answers here and on page 133.

Exercise 4:   ____out of 10 correct

Exercise 5

Say each word in each line below to yourself. Select the word in the line that has the
short sound of *e*. Write that word in the blank space at the right. Say the word again.
Can you hear the short vowel sound of *e* as in *e*gg?

Example: level, reel, heal, kneel____ *level*____

1. web, knee, treat, her____ *web*____
2. sheer, stream, pet, these____ *pet*____
3. bead, scheme, dress, we____ *dress*____
4. spree, trend, weed, were____ *trend*____
5. belt, three, street, dream____ *belt*____

Compare your answers with those given on page 130. Place a checkmark by each of your correct answers. Count the number correct and record that number here and on page 133.

Exercise 5: _____out of 5 correct**

Applying the General Rule to Short E

As you have learned, there is a short vowel sound in most words when a consonant immediately follows the vowel and it is the only vowel in the word. Examples: *sled, shell, nest, spent.*

An exception to this rule for short *e* is when *r* follows the *e*, as in *her, perk, term.* The sound of *e* in such words will be discussed in Chapter 7.

Exercise 6

Using the information you have just learned, complete the following exercise. From this list, select a word with a short *e* sound to complete the sentences below.

peaches	nest	leg	sheep
tree	eggs	three	bench
knee	hen	seat	ten

Example: During the picnic, Ralph fell off the___*bench*___twice.

1. After his home run, the ball player returned to his ___*bench*___.

2. When he opened his lunchbox, he found that the ___*eggs*___ were bad.

3. During the game she scraped her___*leg*___.

4. The bird flew to the ___*nest*___ to feed its young.

5. The farmer's___*hen*___was missing from the barn-yard.

Compare your answers with those given on page 130. Place a checkmark by each of your correct answers. Count the number correct and record that number here and on page 133.

Exercise 6: _____out of 5 correct**

Review Exercise 1

Turn on the skilltape.

Example: led lad <u>lead</u>

1. pat	pet	peat
2. <u>shad</u>	shed	shade
3. mat	met	<u>meet</u>
4. place	please	<u>plank</u>
5. <u>bed</u>	bead	bad
6. man	<u>men</u>	mane
7. bet	bat	<u>beat</u>
8. sat	<u>set</u>	seat
9. tan	ten	teen
10. <u>gat</u>	get	gate

Compare your answers with those given on page 130. Place a checkmark by each of your correct answers. Count the number correct and record that number here and on page 133.

Review Exercise 1: _____out of 10 correct

Review Exercise 2

Change the vowel in each of the following words to *e*. Then substitute a blend or digraph from the list below for the first consonant to make a word. Say the new word. Blends and digraphs: sp, sh, ch, fl, sm, dr, st, sw.

Example: tap ___*step*___

1. band *spend*	6. back *fleck*
2. hall *smell*	7. bad *shed*
3. tall *stall*	8. mast *chest*
4. fast *chest*	9. map *step*
5. mash *flesh*	10. bass *dress*

Compare your answers with those given on page 130. Place a checkmark by each of your correct answers. Count the number correct and record that number here and on page 133.

Review Exercise 2:   _____out of 10 correct

Sound of Short I

Exercise 7

Look at the following two lists of words. The first column contains words that have the long *i* sound. The second column contains words that have the short *i* sound.

Turn on the skilltape.

Long	*Short*
kite	kit
bright	bit
dry	drip
wild	will
grime	grim

Example: _L_

1. __l__ right
2. __s__ prim
3. __l__ light
4. __s__ sit
5. __l__ try

6. __s__ lit
7. __l__ prime
8. __s__ slim
9. __l__ slime
10. __s__ trip

Record the number of correct answers here and on page 133.

Exercise 7:   _____out of 10 correct

Exercise 8

In this exercise, say each word in the line to yourself. Select the word in the line that has the short sound of *i*. Write that word in the blank space at the right. Say the word again. Can you hear the short vowel sound of *i* as in *it*?

Example: lift, tripe, girt, bird____*lift*____

1. scrimp, dirt, flight, mild____*scrimp*____
2. birth, sty, thrift, bride____*thrift*____
3. split, find, first, drive____*split*____
4. flirt, child, might, thrill____*thrill*____
5. shift, thrive, bind, shirt____*shift*____

Compare your answers with those given on page 130. Place a checkmark by each of your correct answers. Count the number correct and record that number here and on page 133.

Exercise 8:   ____out of 5 correct

Recognizing Short I

The sound of *i* is usually short when it is the only vowel in the word and is immediately followed by a consonant. For example, *hip, spit,* and *sprint* have the short vowel sound as in the word *it*.

However, remember that when *i* is followed by -*nd* as in *kind* and *find*, by -*ld* as in *wild* and *child,* and by -*gh* as in *tight* and *might,* the vowel sound of *i* is frequently long. We will discuss the sound of *i* followed by *r* in Chapter 7.

Exercise 9

Select a word with the short *i* sound from the following list to complete the sentences at the top of the next page.

fig	dive	limped	might
prince	pine	cried	ride
swim	knight	will	stick

Example: He needed a *stick* to go hiking in the mountains.

1. The *big* tree had new leaves on it.
2. The *prince* planned to save the lady in distress.
3. Most people like to *swim* in a pool.
4. Sally *limped* because she broke a leg.
5. She *will* enter college next year.

Compare your answers to those given on page 130. Place a checkmark by each of your correct answers. Count the number correct and record that number here and on page 133.

Exercise 9:   _____out of 5 correct

Review Exercise 3

Turn on the skilltape.

(Ed)

Example: <u>itch</u>   irk   ire

1. hat	heat	hit
2. sat	set	sit
3. fan	fin	fine
4. then	thin	than
5. greet	grit	grab
6. tan	tin	ten
7. bet	bit	bat
8. mat	mit	met
9. sheen	shin	shall
10. mad	mid	med

Compare your answers with those given on page 130. Place a checkmark by each of your correct answers. Count the number correct and record that number here and on page 133.

Review Exercise 3:   _____out of 10 correct

Review Exercise 4

Change the vowel in each word to *i*. Then substitute a blend or digraph for the initial consonant or consonant blend. Say the new word to yourself. Use these blends and digraphs: sp, sh, ch, fl, sm, dr, st, gr, str, spl.

Examples: map *flip*
pen *chin*

1. bent _____
2. rap_____
3. fall _____
4. ham_____
5. hen_____

6. check_____
7. chat _____
8. black_____
9. smell_____
10. span_____

Compare your answers with those given on page 130. Place a checkmark by each of your correct answers. Count the number correct and record that number here and on page 133.

Review Exercise 4: _____out of 10 correct

Turn on Skilltape 6, side B.

Sound of Short O

Exercise 10

Look at the following two lists of words. The first column contains words that have the long *o* sound. The second column contains words that have the short *o* sound.

Turn on the skilltape.

Long	*Short*
coat	cot
road	rod
code	cod
hope	hop
wrote	rot

Example: _Δ_

1. _____   6. _____

2. _____   7. _____

3. _____   8. _____

4. _____   9. _____

5. _____   10. _____

Record the number of correct answers here and on page 133.

Exercise 10:   _____ out of 10 correct

Exercise 11

In this exercise, say each word in the line to yourself. Select the word in the line that has the short sound of *o*. Write that word in the blank at the right. Say the word again. Can you hear the short vowel sound of *o* as in *on?*

Example: tone, ton, tool, tot_____ *tot* _____

1. close, roll, sport, blot _____

2. broke, scorch, shock, flow_____

3. float, blond, gold, bore_____

4. fold, rope, goes, drop_____

5. coach, stone, chop, tore_____

Compare your answers with those given on page 131. Place a checkmark by each of your correct answers. Count the number of correct answers and record that number here and on page 133.

Exercise 11:   _____ out of 5 correct

Recognizing Short O

The sound of *o* is usually short when it is the only vowel in a word and it is immediately followed by a consonant. For example, *hop, stock,* and *spot* have the short vowel sound as in the word *on.*

However, remember that when *o* is followed by *l,* as in *cold, told,* and *fold* the vowel sound of *o* is frequently long. We will discuss the sound of *o* followed by *r* in Chapter 7.

Exercise 12

From the following list, select a word with the short *o* sound to complete each of the sentences below.

stone	rock	bowl	fox
hot	logs	box	trot
coal	cold	colt	stroll

Example: The group took off on an easy___*trot*___.

1. The scientist found a rare_____on his trip.

2. Joe put a_____of cereal on the table.

3. Mother said the food was so_____that she could not eat it.

4. The man put_____in the fireplace.

5. The_____ran through the field.

Compare your answers with those given on page 131. Place a checkmark by each of your correct answers. Count the number correct and record that number here and on page 133.

Exercise 12: ____out of 5 correct

Review Exercise 5

Turn on the skilltape.

Example: limp lamp loam <u>lent</u>

1.	laid	load	led	lead
2.	stop	step	steep	stint
3.	crab	crib	cod	creep
4.	shop	ship	sharp	sheep
5.	rise	rose	raise	rest
6.	black	block	belch	blind
7.	role	rule	real	rail
8.	rode	ride	reed	red
9.	wide	wed	weed	wade
10.	road	reed	ride	rid

Compare your answers with those given on page 131. Place a checkmark by each of your correct answers. Count the number correct and record that number here and page 133.

Review Exercise 5: ____out of 10 correct

Review Exercise 6

Change the vowel in each of the following words to *o*. Then substitute a blend or digraph for the initial consonant or consonant blend. Say the new word to yourself. Use these blends and digraphs: sh, sc, tr, ch, sm, dr, st, sp, cl, gl, gr.

Examples: trip *chop*
sat *blot*

1. chat_____
2. stitch_____
3. bled_____
4. dad_____
5. strip_____

6. pat_____
7. fig_____
8. back_____
9. step_____
10. tick_____

Compare your answers with those given on page 131. Place a checkmark by each of your correct answers. Count the number correct and record it here and on page 133.

Review Exercise 6: ____out of 10 correct

Sound of Short U

Exercise 13

Look at the two following lists of words. The first column contains words that have the long *u* sound. The second column contains words that have the short *u* sound.

Turn on the skilltape.

Long	Short
cube	cub
cute	cut
mule	must
huge	hug
fume	fun

Example: _△_

1. ___	6. ___
2. ___	7. ___
3. ___	8. ___
4. ___	9. ___
5. ___	10. ___

Record the number of correct answers here and on page 133.

Exercise 13:   _____out of 10 correct**

Exercise 14

For this exercise, say each word in the following lines to yourself. Select that word in each line that has the short sound of *u*. Write that word in the blank at the right. Say the word again. Can you hear the short vowel sound of *u* as in *up?*

Example: dune, ruin, run, road____ *run* ____

1. huge, hunt, fuel, pew_____

2. chuck, rule, stew, cube_____

3. strum, few, mule, duel_____

4. fuse, dew, trump, fur_____

5. flue, new, strut, burn_____

Compare your answers with those given on page 131. Place a checkmark by each of your correct answers. Then count the number correct and record that number here and on page 133.

Exercise 14:   _____out of 5 correct**

Exercise 15

From the following list of words, select a word with the short *u* sound to complete each of the sentences below.

mule	drum	feud	use
cut	lunches	cubes	duck
gun	fume	fuss	flute

Example: The _*lunches*_ weren't ready to eat yet.

1. The_____was tied up in the barnyard.

2. Do not_____the newspaper for scrap until everyone has read it.

3. He learned to play the_____in the school band.

4. The noise of the_____woke him from a deep sleep.

5. Mary did not_____over the mistake.

Compare your answers with those given on page 131. Place a checkmark by each of your correct answers. Then count the number correct and record that number here and on page 133.

Exercise 15: _____ out of 5 correct

Review Exercise 7

Turn on the skilltape.

Example: cheat chair <u>chest</u> chip chop

1. hug	hag	hip	hep	hop
2. mud	mid	med	mad	mod
3. shut	shot	chat	cheat	chin
4. rut	root	rat	rip	red
5. fuel	full	fill	fell	fall
6. tell	till	tall	toll	tuck
7. trump	track	trick	trend	trod
8. stump	stomp	stamp	stem	stint
9. ran	wren	rut	rot	rich
10. shred	shrank	shrik	shrunk	shone

Compare your answers to those given on page 131. Place a checkmark by each of your correct answers. Then count the number correct and record that number here and on page 133.

Review Exercise 7: _____out of 10 correct

Review Exercise 8

Change the vowel in each of the following words to *u*. Then substitute a blend or digraph for the initial consonant or consonant blend. Say the new word to yourself. Use these blends and digraphs in your answers: st, br, str, dr, cl, thr, th, cr, bl.

Examples: stamp *thump*
stitch *crutch*

1. brat_____ 6. pitch_____
2. spent_____ 7. blast_____
3. pant_____ 8. hemp_____
4. ham_____ 9. cinch_____
5. hedge_____ 10. splash_____

Compare your answers with those on page 131. Place a checkmark by each of your correct answers. Then count the number correct and record that number here and on page 133.

Review Exercise 8: _____out of 10 correct

Review Exercise 9

Using the knowledge you have gained about long and short vowels, underline the vowel or vowel combination in the nonsense words below. Mark *L* if the vowel sound you underlined is long, or *S* if the vowel sound is short.

Examples: spl<u>o</u>p *S*
b<u>i</u>ld *L*

1. stold____ 6. drost____ 11. mune____ 16. zold____
2. chup____ 7. rees____ 12. thaid____ 17. drech____
3. clayd____ 8. stry____ 13. stram____ 18. mete____
4. stom____ 9. crump____ 14. chine____ 19. braf____
5. drabe____ 10. chent____ 15. thrit____ 20. leat____

Compare your answers with those on page 131. Place a checkmark by each of your correct answers (each number has two parts). Then count the number correct and record that number here and on page 133.

Review Exercise 9:   _____out of 40 correct

Review Exercise 10

Look at the following words and pronounce them to yourself: *as, egg, it, on, up.* These words with short vowel sounds will help you in the following exercise.

Turn on the skilltape.

Example: _____*tut*_____ *u*

1. _____ ____   6. _____ ____
2. _____ ____   7. _____ ____
3. _____ ____   8. _____ ____
4. _____ ____   9. _____ ____
5. _____ ____   10. _____ ____

Record the numbers of correct answers here and on page 133.

Review Exercise 10:   _____out of 20 correct

P
O
S
T
T
E
S
T
S

Posttest A

Turn on the skilltape.

Example: _ı̇_

1. ____   5. ____   9. ____   13. ____   17. ____

2. ____   6. ____   10. ____   14. ____   18. ____

3. ____   7. ____   11. ____   15. ____   19. ____

4. ____   8. ____   12. ____   16. ____   20. ____

Posttest B

Using a short vowel, complete the word in parentheses and write it in the blank so the sentence will make sense.

Example: Lois carried the shopping____*bag*____to the car. (b_*a*_g)

1. The baseball player could not_____the ball. (h____t)

2. The policeman's_____was silver. (b____dge)

3. Animals like to hide in_____of trees. (cl____mps)

4. The weightlifter could not_____the barbell. (l____ft)

5. The wrestler was pinned to the_____. (m____t)

6. The owner threw a_____to her dog. (st____ck)

7. The tramp fell asleep in his_____. (sh____ck)

8. Joel will_____the vegetables in the food processor. (bl____nd)

9. Linda will have to_____to reach the apples on the tree. (str____tch)

10. From_____to dawn the city was quiet. (d____sk)

Compare your answers to these posttests with those on page 132. Place a checkmark by the number of each of your correct answers. Count the number correct for each posttest and record your score here and on page 133.

Posttest A: ____out of 20 correct
Posttest B: ____out of 10 correct
Total: ____out of 30 correct

If you got 27 or more correct, you can go on to the next chapter and take the pretests as directed.

If you got less than 27 correct, talk with your instructor.

Show your instructor the summary sheet on page 133 on which you have recorded your scores for all the exercises and tests.

Answers to Exercises Not on the Skilltape

Exercise 2

1. lack   2. flap   3. band   4. black   5. slat

Exercise 3

1. camp   2. hands   3. black   4. bass   5. pan

Exercise 5

1. web   2. pet   3. dress   4. trend   5. belt

Exercise 6

1. bench   2. eggs   3. leg   4. nest   5. hen

Review Exercise 1

1. pet   3. meet   5. bed   7. beat   9. tan
2. shad   4. plank   6. men   8. set   10. gat

Review Exercise 2

1. spend   3. spell, swell,   5. flesh   7. shed, sped,   9. step
2. spell, swell,   shell, smell   6. speck, fleck,   fled   10. dress, chess
   shell, smell   4. chest   check   8. chest

Exercise 8

1. scrimp   2. thrift   3. split   4. thrill   5. shift

Exercise 9

1. fig   2. prince   3. swim   4. limped   5. will

Review Exercise 3

1. hit   3. fine   5. grit   7. bat   9. sheen
2. set   4. thin   6. ten   8. met   10. mid

Review Exercise 4

1. flint, splint, stint   6. flick, stick, chick
2. strip, chip, flip, grip, drip, ship   7. spit, split, grit, chit, flit
3. drill, chill, shill, still, spill, grill   8. (same as 6)
4. flim, grim, shim   9. (same as 3)
5. spin, chin, grin, shin   10. (same as 5)

Exercise 11

1. blot   2. shock   3. blond   4. drop   5. chop

Exercise 12

1. rock   2. box   3. hot   4. logs   5. fox

Review Exercise 5

1. led	3. cod	5. rise	7. real	9. weed
2. step	4. ship	6. block	8. red	10. rid

Review Exercise 6

1. shot, trot, spot, scot, clot
2. scotch
3. shod, clod, trod
4. (same as 3)
5. glop, stop, shop, chop, drop, clop

6. (same as 1)
7. smog, clog, grog
8. clock, shock, smock, stock, chock
9. (same as 5)
10. (same as 8)

Exercise 14

1. hunt   2. chuck   3. strum   4. trump   5. strut

Exercise 15

1. duck   2. cut   3. drum   4. gun   5. fuss

Review Exercise 7

1. hep	3. shot	5. fill	7. trend	9. rot
2. mid	4. rut	6. tuck	8. stump	10. shrunk

Review Exercise 8

1. strut
2. stunt, brunt, blunt
3. (same as 2)
4. drum, strum, thrum
5. drudge

6. clutch, crutch
7. thrust, crust
8. thump, clump, stump
9. brunch, crunch
10. blush, brush, thrush, crush

Review Exercise 9

1. stold, L	5. drabe, L	9. crump, S	13. stram, S	17. drech, S
2. chup, S	6. drost, S	10. chent, S	14. chine, L	18. mete, L
3. clayd, L	7. rees, L	11. mune, L	15. thrit, S	19. braf, S
4. stom, S	8. stry, L	12. thaid, L	16. zold, L	20. leat, L

Answers to Pretests and Posttests

Pretest A

1. e	5. e	9. i	13. e	17. u
2. a	6. a	10. u	14. a	18. o
3. i	7. o	11. a	15. i	19. u
4. o	8. e	12. a	16. o	20. e

Pretest B

1. cab	3. plum	4. swim	5. rock	6. ten
2. hat				

Posttest A

1. a	5. o	9. o	13. u	17. i
2. i	6. a	10. u	14. e	18. e
3. u	7. i	11. i	15. a	19. a
4. e	8. e	12. u	16. a	20. u

Posttest B

1. hit	3. clumps	5. mat	7. shack	9. stretch
2. badge	4. lift	6. stick	8. blend	10. dusk

SUMMARY SHEET

Chapter 6

Record your scores for each test and exercise.

	Number Correct	**Instructor's Comments**
Pretest A	_____out of 20 correct	
Pretest B	_____out of 6 correct	
Exercise 1	_____out of 10 correct	
Exercise 2	_____out of 5 correct	
Exercise 3	_____out of 5 correct	
Exercise 4	_____out of 10 correct	
Exercise 5	_____out of 5 correct	
Exercise 6	_____out of 5 correct	
Review Exercise 1	_____out of 10 correct	
Review Exercise 2	_____out of 10 correct	
Exercise 7	_____out of 10 correct	
Exercise 8	_____out of 5 correct	
Exercise 9	_____out of 5 correct	
Review Exercise 3	_____out of 10 correct	
Review Exercise 4	_____out of 10 correct	
Exercise 10	_____out of 10 correct	
Exercise 11	_____out of 5 correct	
Exercise 12	_____out of 5 correct	
Review Exercise 5	_____out of 10 correct	
Review Exercise 6	_____out of 10 correct	
Exercise 13	_____out of 10 correct	
Exercise 14	_____out of 5 correct	
Exercise 15	_____out of 5 correct	
Review Exercise 7	_____out of 10 correct	
Review Exercise 8	_____out of 10 correct	
Review Exercise 9	_____out of 40 correct	
Review Exercise 10	_____out of 20 correct	
Posttest A	_____out of 20 correct	
Posttest B	_____out of 10 correct	

7

Varying Vowels

Glossary

Vowel Digraphs: two vowels that come together and represent only one vowel sound, such as the *ea* in *heat,* *oa* in *boat,* *au* in *haul,* and *oo* in *soon.*

Vowel Diphthongs: the vowel combinations of *oi* as in *oil,* *oy* as in *boy,* *ou* as in *out* and *ow* as in *owl.*

R-controlled Vowels: are vowel sounds that are neither long nor short but are influenced or controlled by the letter *r,* as the *a* in the words *car* and *care.*

Introduction

So far you have learned about long and short vowels. Many words in our language have other vowel sounds. This chapter is about these varying vowel sounds. When you finish working through this chapter, you will be able to recognize and pronounce *vowel digraphs* when they stand for long sounds as well as other sounds. You will also learn about the *vowel diphthongs* along with those vowel sounds controlled by the letters *r* and *l* in certain words. The concept of the letters *w* and *y* as vowels and the vowel combination *ie/ei* in words is also a part of this chapter.

Use Skilltape 7 to help you work through this chapter. The directions in this worktext will tell you when to turn on the skilltape.

The next section contains the pretests for Chapter 7. To see how much of the material in this chapter you already know, go now to Pretests A, B, and C. Complete each to the best of your ability.

Pretest A

Turn on Skilltape 7, side A.

Example: float <u>flout</u>

1. bloat	bleat	6. lawn	loan
2. creek	croak	7. shook	shock
3. clawed	cloud	8. pall	pool
4. broil	brawl	9. clean	clown
5. shoot	shout	10. fault	felt

Pretest B

Turn on the skilltape.

1. bar	bare	6. chalk	check
2. fir	fire	7. cull	call
3. sire	sir	8. halt	hilt
4. purr	pure	9. star	stare
5. firm	farm	10. fear	fur

Pretest C

Place a vowel digraph or diphthong in each blank space below to make a word. Use the following combinations: *ea, ee, au, aw, ay, ai, ou, ow, oa, oo, oi, oy*. Then pronounce the word to yourself.

Example: pl_ea_

1. fl____t	6. b____l	11. sh____t	16. v____lt
2. dr____m	7. cl____t	12. cr____k	17. thr____t
3. bl____k	8. st____n	13. h____f	18. b____
4. h____l	9. str____	14. ____l	19. t____l
5. sh____l	10. r____d	15. thr____	20. str____t

Compare your answers to these pretests with those on page 159. Place a checkmark by each of your correct answers. Count the number correct for each pretest and write that number in the space provided here and on page 160.

Pretest A: _____out of 10 correct
Pretest B: _____out of 10 correct
Pretest C: _____out of 20 correct
Total: _____out of 40 correct

If you got 36 or more correct, you may go on to the posttests on pages 155–56.
If you got less than 36 correct, complete this chapter and then take the posttests.

Vowel Digraphs

A *vowel digraph* is two vowels together that make one sound. For example, *boat,* *feel, pay, paid,* and *plead* contain vowel digraphs. In these words, the first vowel of the digraph is long and the second vowel is silent.

Exercise 1

Turn on the skilltape.

Examples: cot _S_   coat _L_

1. goat _l_	got _s_	7. bat _s_	bait _l_
2. pet _s_	meat _l_	8. say _l_	sad _s_
3. lad _s_	laid _l_	9. boat _l_	hot _s_
4. hay _l_	had _s_	10. fled _s_	fleet _l_
5. float _l_	trot _s_	11. pail _l_	pal _s_
6. street _l_	fret _s_	12. stray _l_	glad _s_

Record the number of correct answers here and on page 160.

Exercise 1: ____out of 24 correct

Exercise 2

All of the words in this exercise contain vowel digraphs. Cross out the *silent* vowel and write the letter of the long vowel sound in the space provided. Then pronounce the word to yourself.

Example: sail _a_

1. road____	6. gait____	11. toad____	16. trait____
2. frail____	7. flail____	12. bait____	17. raid____
3. wheel____	8. bloat____	13. steel____	18. play____
4. loaf____	9. greet____	14. coach____	19. roast____
5. tray____	10. nail____	15. screech____	20. leech____

Compare your answers with those given on page 157. Place a checkmark by each of your correct answers (each number has two parts). Count the number correct and record that number here and on page 160.

Exercise 2: ____out of 40 correct

The Digraph EA

The digraph *ea* has two common vowel sounds. The most common sound of the digraph *ea* is long *e*, as in *feats, treat, meal,* and *peach.* The other common sound is short *e*, as in *bread, dread, breath,* and *sweat.* Another less common sound is when the *e* is silent and the *a* is long, as in the word *great.*

Exercise 3

Turn on the skilltape.

Examples: leave *long e*
bread *short e*
great *long a*

1. stream *le*
2. spread *la*
3. steak *la*
4. breath *se*
5. scream *le*

6. break *la*
7. head *se*
8. teach *le*
9. thread *se*
10. tease *le*

Record the number of correct answers here and on page 160.

Exercise 3: ____out of 10 correct

Exercise 4

The following words contain vowel digraphs in which the first vowel is long and the second is silent. Write the letter that represents the long vowel sound in the space provided. Then pronounce the word to yourself.

Example: leak   _ℓ_

1. streak_ℓ_   6. plead_ℓ_
2. goat_ℓ_   7. soap_ℓ_
3. fleece_ℓ_   8. strait_ℓ_
4. braid_ℓ_   9. scream_ℓ_
5. pray_ℓ_   10. broach_ℓ_

Compare your answers with those given on page 157. Place a checkmark by each of your correct answers. Count the number correct and record that number here and on page 160.

Exercise 4:   ____out of 10 correct

Other Vowel Digraphs

There are a few vowel digraphs that are frequent and consistent in sound. Some examples of these are the *au* in *haul, aw* in *flaw, oo* in *food,* and *oo* in *book.* In these words, the vowels do not follow the rule that you learned for long first vowel, silent second vowel. The first vowel is *not* long in these digraphs, *nor* is the second one silent. These vowel combinations make a new sound. Look at the following patterns: cat—caw, pan—paw, at—all, was—wall, dance—dawn. When *l* and *w* follow *a, a* is changed to the sound found in *paw* and *all. Au* in the word *sauce* has the same sound as *aw* in *paw* and *al* in *call.*

Exercise 5

Turn on the skilltape.

Key words: bat   base   paw   haul

Example: _X_

1. ____   6. ____
2. ____   7. ____
3. ____   8. ____
4. ____   9. ____
5. ____   10. ____

Record the number of correct answers here and on page 160.

Exercise 5: _____out of 10 correct

Exercise 6

Look at the following list of words. After the first word in each line there are several other words. Say all the words to yourself. Find and underline that word in the line that has the same vowel sound that the first word has.

Example: saw   rate   <u>haul</u>   strand   card

1. claw	<u>tall</u>	cheat	flay	bask
2. salt	roast	reap	tram	<u>maul</u>
3. call	charm	made	<u>thaw</u>	flake
4. haul	float	<u>brawl</u>	braid	break
5. thaw	black	trade	<u>fault</u>	trek
6. hall	bread	damp	<u>sprawl</u>	boast
7. draw	<u>launch</u>	leap	spray	creek
8. straw	cheese	<u>stalk</u>	pride	bowl
9. taught	beat	street	blank	<u>stall</u>
10. bawl	bench	coach	<u>flaunt</u>	fleet

Compare your answers with those given on page 157. Place a checkmark by each of your correct answers. Count the number correct and record that number here and on page 160.

Exercise 6: _____out of 10 correct

In Exercise 6 you studied the vowel sound found in the word *paw*. This sound is also found in words that are spelled differently. Look at these words:

paw	haul	salt	all	walk
claw	sauce	halt	call	talk
flaw	maul	malt	mall	chalk

Sounds of Double O

Look at this word: *rot*. Now notice the word *root*. Are the vowel sounds in both words the same? As you say the words to yourself, can you hear the difference: *Rot* has a short *o* sound and *root* has the sound of double *o* as in *moon*. The following exercise will give you practice in hearing the double *o* sound.

Exercise 7

Turn on the skilltape.

Key words: look book food moon

Example: __*o*__

1. ____   6. ____
2. ____   7. ____
3. ____   8. ____
4. ____   9. ____
5. ____   10. ____

Record the number of correct answers here and on page 160.

Exercise 7: ____out of 10 correct

Exercise 8

For each word in this exercise, substitute a single consonant, blend, or digraph for the initial consonant or blend. Then change the vowel *o* to double *o* to make a new word. Use a different word for each exercise. The new word must have the same vowel sound you hear in the word *moon*. Pronounce each new word to yourself.

Example: rot __*shoot*__

1. hot__*hoot*__   4. drop__*droop*__
2. hop__*hoop*__   5. mod__*mood*__
3. shot__*shoot*__

Compare your answers with those given on page 157. Place a checkmark by each of your correct answers. Count the number correct and record that number here and on page 160.

Exercise 8: _____out of 5 correct

Say the word *lock*. Then say the word *look*. Are the vowel sounds the same in both words? As you say the words to yourself, can you hear the difference? *Lock* has a short *o* sound and *look* has the sound of double *o* you hear in *book*.

Exercise 9

For each of the following sentences, select that word in italic type that has the same vowel sound you hear in *book*. Write that word in the space provided at the right.

Example: The *cook* used a *stool* to reach the top shelf.   ___*cook*___

1. The *food* is very *good*.   _____

2. She put her *foot* in the *boot*.   _____

3. The woman *shook* her *broom*.   _____

4. The man *stood* up and walked across the *room*.   _____

5. The *cook* stirred the stew with a *spoon*.   _____

Compare your answers with those given on page 157. Place a checkmark by each of your correct answers. Count the number correct and record it here and on page 160.

Exercise 9: _____out of 5 correct

Exercise 10

Turn on the skilltape.

Example: <u>loose</u>   spool   <u>good</u>

1. gloom   choose   foot

2. spook   nook   cook

3. spool   shook   noon

4. smooth   hook   book

5. good   broom   soothe

Record the number of correct answers here and on page 160.

Exercise 10: _____out of 10 correct

Exercise 11

gold	smooth	wood	blotch
odd	brook	toll	stone
clock	foot	choose	room

For each key word below, select three words from the list above that have the same vowel sound and write them in the spaces. Use each word only once.

1. go   _gold_   _told_   _stone_

2. book _foot_   _wood_   _brook_

3. food _smooth_ _choose_ _room_

4. cot   _odd_   _clock_   _blotch_

Compare your answers with those on page 157. Place a checkmark by each of your correct answers. Count the number correct and record that number here and on page 160. Each word counts as one correct answer.

Diphthongs

Diphthongs are combinations of vowel sounds similar to digraphs. Digraphs, you remember, are two vowels that make one distinct vowel sound, such as the *ea* in *beat.* In *beat,* the *e* is long and the *a* is silent. In diphthongs, the two vowels seem to merge as the *o* and *i* do in *oil.* You can almost hear two vowels in this word. The common diphthongs are *oi* and *oy,* as in *oil* and *boy* and *ou* and *ow,* as in *shout* and *cow.*

Exercise 12

Turn on Skilltape 7, side B.

Key words:　oil　boil　boy　toy

Example:　__X__

1. ____　　　　　　6. ____

2. ____　　　　　　7. ____

3. ____　　　　　　8. ____

4. ____　　　　　　9. ____

5. ____　　　　　　10. ____

Record the number of correct answers here and on page 160.

Exercise 12:　____out of 10 correct

Exercise 13

Say each of the following words to yourself. Underline those words that have the same vowel sound that you hear in *oil*.

1. soy　　　　　6. coy　　　　　11. sprawl

2. draw　　　　7. trail　　　　12. spoil

3. choice　　　8. broil　　　　13. jaunt

4. lawn　　　　9. float　　　　14. joint

5. real　　　　10. joy　　　　　15. coin

Compare your answers with those given on page 157. Place a checkmark by each of your correct answers. Count the number correct and record that number here and on page 160.

Exercise 13:　____out of 15 correct

In the previous exercises, you learned that *oi* and *oy* always sound the same. Although *oi* and *oy* sound the same, *oy* is frequently found at the end of small words. *Oi* is usually found in the middle of small words or sometimes at the beginning of small words.

oi	*oy*
foil	boy
spoil	coy
loin	joy
point	toy
oil	ploy

OU and OW

Unlike *oi* and *oy* which are consistent in sound, *ou* and *ow* have several sounds. Look at these words and pronounce them to yourself: *out, cow, rob*. Which of these words contain the same vowel sound? *Out* and *cow* have the same vowel sound. This is the most common sound of *ou* and *ow*.

Exercise 14

Turn on the skilltape.

Key words: out   scout   cow   how

Examples: __X__   ____

1. ____ ____   6. ____ ____

2. ____ ____   7. ____ ____

3. ____ ____   8. ____ ____

4. ____ ____   9. ____ ____

5. ____ ____   10. ____ ____

Exercise 14:   ____out of 15 correct

Exercise 15

Look at the following list of words. After the first word in each line, there are several other words. Say the words to yourself. Find the word that has the same vowel sound as the first word and underline it.

Example: loud   gout   grow   got

1. down	shout	coat	box
2. boat	out	snow	clock
3. trout	float	how	jaw
4. crowd	grow	gold	growl
5. drop	shock	flow	shout
6. round	soap	vouch	spoil
7. clown	low	all	spout
8. deep	clean	cliff	cleft
9. walk	plow	thaw	mow
10. toil	bowl	spouse	ploy

Compare your answers with those on page 157. Place a checkmark by each of your correct answers. Count the number correct and record that number here and on page 160.

Exercise 15: _____out of 10 correct

The Other Sound of OW

Look at the following words and pronounce them: *clown, snow*. What vowel sound do you hear in *snow*? *Snow* has the long vowel sound of *o*. The *ow* in *clown* has the same vowel sound as the *ou* in *out*. The following chart may help you to recognize the different sounds of *ow*.

Key word: clown	Key word: snow
down	grow
crowd	low
drown	tow
gown	flow
frown	bowl

Suggestion: to help you pronounce words with *ow*, try both pronunciations to see which one is familiar.

The Other Sound of OU

Look at the following words and pronounce them: *bound, touch*. What vowel sound do you hear in *bound*? What vowel sound do you hear in *touch*? Are they the same? *Pound* has the same vowel sound found in the words *out* and *cow*. *Touch* has a short *u* sound, like the *u* in *much* and *rust*.

Key word: touch	Key word: bound
rough	round
tough	ground
double	shroud
young	sprout

Exercise 16

Turn on the skilltape.

Example: blouse   grow   <u>cow</u>   sound

1. stout	<u>pound</u>	town	foil
2. mouse	croak	<u>frown</u>	<u>brown</u>
3. flee	<u>street</u>	croak	frail
4. fraud	fear	<u>haul</u>	cow
5. proud	<u>gown</u>	stroke	shop
6. crown	<u>cloud</u>	<u>mouth</u>	<u>trout</u>
7. know	<u>mow</u>	growl	grout
8. young	mall	moat	<u>must</u>
9. brow	<u>snout</u>	rough	bowl
10. ounce	oil	all	<u>louse</u>

Compare your answers with those on page 158. Place a checkmark by each of your correct answers. Count the number correct and record that number here and on page 160.

Exercise 16: ____**out of 14 correct**

Exercise 17

Turn on the skilltape.

	Long o sound show	*Short u sound* touch	*ou/ow sound* ouch, down
Example:	X	___	___
1.	___	___	___
2.	___	___	___
3.	___	___	___
4.	___	___	___
5.	___	___	___
6.	___	___	___
7.	___	___	___
8.	___	___	___
9.	___	___	___
10.	___	___	___

Record the number of correct answers here and on page 160.

Exercise 17:   ____out of 10 correct

R-controlled Vowels

Another vowel variation in small words is the r-controlled sound. When *r* immediately follows a vowel, the sound of the vowel is quite different than when the vowel stands alone. For instance, *pat* and *part* have quite different sounds as a result of the *r* sound being added. In most small words containing *er, ir,* and *ur,* the sound you hear with these combinations is the same sound you hear in the word *her.*

Exercise 18

Turn on the skilltape.

	car	*for*	*herd*
Example:	___	___	X

	car	*for*	*her*
1.	____	____	____
2.	____	____	____
3.	____	____	____
4.	____	____	____
5.	____	____	____
6.	____	____	____
7.	____	____	____
8.	____	____	____
9.	____	____	____
10.	____	____	____

Compare your answers with those given on page 158. Place a checkmark by each of your correct answers. Count the number correct and record that number here and on page 160.

Exercise 18:   ____out of 10 correct

Other R-controlled Sounds

The sound that you hear in the word *care* is found in several vowel combinations, as in *bare, bear,* and *hair*. Table 1 illustrates most of the common words with that vowel sound.

Table 1

Other R-controlled Sounds

bare	*bear*	*hair*
care	pear	pair
dare	wear	fair
fare	tear	air
hare	swear	flair
mare		stair
pare		lair
rare		
ware		
flare		
scare		
share		
snare		
square		
stare		

The vowel combination -*ear* has two other sounds. To be sure of pronunciation, it is best to learn the few words that contain this combination. Study Table 2.

Table 2

Sounds of -EAR

-ear as in dear	*-ear as in her*
fear	earn
beard	pearl
clear	search
shear	learn
ear	early
gear	heard
hear	
smear	
tear	

IE/EI

There is sometimes much confusion about pronouncing words with the vowel combinations *ie* and *ei*. However, there is a simple way of learning the sounds. You should remember that in most words that have the *ie* combination, the vowel sound is long *e*, as in *grief*. Table 3 shows you many of the words with the *ie* combination. In a few cases the *ie* has the long sound of *i* as in *tie*.

Table 3

Sounds of IE

ie, long e as in grief		*ie, long i as in tie*	
thief	siege	die	fried
piece	wield	pie	tied
chief	tier	lie	cried
brief	fierce	dried	spied
yield	pier	lied	
niece	field		
shield	priest		
pierce			

The *ei* combination has two popular sounds. It has the long *e* sound in very few words, such as *weird*. The most popular sound is long *a* as illustrated in this brief list: *reign, eight, neigh, weight, rein, sleigh, freight, vein, weigh.*

Other Vowel Combinations

There are many other vowel combinations that make different sounds. Because there are so many and they appear so rarely, there is no reason for you to learn them now. When you come across them, you may have to use other skills in order to sound them out. However, there are several vowel combinations that appear frequently enough to mention. Table 4 shows these combinations, how they sound, and some of the common words in which they are found.

Table 4

Less Common Vowel Combinations

igh (long i)	ew (long u)	ew (long oo)	ue (long u)	ue (long oo)
sight	few	grew	due*	true
might	dew*	flew	cue	blue
tight	stew*	screw	hue	clue
right	new*	blew		
light	hew	crew		
night	pew	brew		
		drew		
		chew*		

*May be pronounced with long *u* or long *oo*. A good principle to remember is that when a blend or digraph comes before the vowel combination *ue* or *ew*, the long *oo* is correct and in many cases is the only way it could be pronounced. Because of the *l* and *r*, the long *u* sound is impossible to pronounce.

Another vowel combination that is seen frequently but which is very inconsistent is *ough*. Table 5 contains common words with *ough* that should be memorized.

Table 5

Words with -OUGH

ough (long o)	ough (aw)	ough (long oo)	ough (awf)	ough (uf)	ough (ou)
dough	thought	through	cough	tough	bough
though	bought			rough	
	brought				
	fought				

Where simple words end with a final *y*, the *y* sounds like a long *i* as in by.

fry	try	pry	why
sly	sky	fly	cry
dry	shy	sty	ply
my	spy	by	wry

Vowel Review

In this exercise, there are 20 nonsense words. Find the word in each line that has the same vowel sound as the first word in the line and underline it.

Example: strote   strout   <u>stroat</u>   stroit

1. trawl	<u>shaw</u>	shoy	drow
2. blate	bleet	staut	<u>skaid</u>
3. froid	cawd	<u>croy</u>	frode
4. trowd	cort	<u>blouk</u>	floab
5. clowt	troil	bauk	<u>brouch</u>
6. strete	<u>cleet</u>	flate	brite
7. blay	bleek	<u>prade</u>	broid
8. flaid	sreak	clount	<u>draze</u>
9. bawd	boud	<u>baud</u>	boid
10. fule	chout	<u>mube</u>	stroy
11. strad	<u>chast</u>	stred	chost
12. plotch	plote	brack	<u>hok</u>
13. bresh	fraish	brist	<u>gled</u>
14. gund	<u>cust</u>	gaund	gond
15. grich	splech	<u>nitch</u>	splatch
16. strout	flowt	croin	blook
17. brall	flouch	dreach	<u>shalk</u>
18. foost	floud	<u>slooch</u>	braut
19. beel	crast	blick	<u>cleak</u>
20. stoab	<u>doub</u>	pold	bauch

Compare your answers with those given on page 158. Place a checkmark by each of your correct answers. Count the number correct and record that number here and on page 160.

Vowel Review: _____out of 20 correct

Posttest A

Turn on the skilltape.

Example: preen <u>prawn</u>

1. clean	clown	6. brood	broad
2. lean	loan	7. foil	fowl
3. peal	pool	8. brawn	brown
4. sweet	sweat	9. crook	croak
5. bread	breed	10. spoil	spool

Posttest B

Turn on the skilltape.

1. her	hear	6. car	care
2. form	farm	7. chalk	chock
3. shell	shall	8. shirt	short
4. coal	call	9. mull	mall
5. bear	beer	10. poor	pore

Posttest C

Place a vowel digraph or diphthong in each blank space below to make a word. Use the following combinations: ea, ee, ay, ai, oa, ow, au, aw, oo, oi, oy, ou.

Example: sw_*ee*_t

1. sw____p	6. t____el
2. f____lt	7. gr____ch
3. scr____m	8. sp____l
4. str____	9. bl____se
5. cl____m	10. j____nt

11. fl___nt   16. spr___

12. br___   17. s___nt

13. cr___k   18. sh___k

14. st___   19. ch___se

15. cl___k   20. pr___ch

Compare your answers to these posttests with those on page 159. Place a checkmark by each of your correct answers. Count the number correct for each posttest and record your score here and on page 160.

Posttest A: ___out of 10 correct
Posttest B: ___out of 10 correct
Posttest C: ___out of 20 correct
Total: ___out of 40 correct

If you got 36 or more correct, you can go on to the next chapter and take the pretests as directed.
If you got less than 36 correct, talk with your instructor.
Show your instructor the summary sheet on page 160 on which you have recorded your scores for all the exercises and tests.

Answers to Exercises Not on the Skilltape

Exercise 2

1. road, o	5. tray, a	9. greet, e	13. steel, e	17. raid, a
2. frail, a	6. gait, a	10. nail, a	14. coach, o	18. play, a
3. wheel, e	7. flail, a	11. toad, o	15. screech, e	19. roast, o
4. loaf, o	8. bloat, o	12. bait, a	16. trait, a	20. leech, e

Exercise 4

1. e	3. e	5. a	7. o	9. e
2. o	4. a	6. e	8. a	10. o

Exercise 6

1. tall	3. thaw	5. fault	7. launch	9. stall
2. maul	4. brawl	6. sprawl	8. stalk	10. flaunt

Exercise 8

These are only some of the possible answers. If you do not find your answer here, check a dictionary. Be sure the double *o* has the sound you hear in *moon*.

1. shoot, loot, boot
2. droop, troop, sloop
3. hoot, boot, loot
4. troop, hoop, sloop
5. food

Exercise 9

1. good	2. foot	3. shook	4. stood	5. cook

Exercise 11

1. gold, toll, stone
2. brook, foot, wood
3. smooth, choose, room
4. odd, clock, blotch

Exercise 13

These words should be underlined: soy, choice, coy, broil, joy, spoil, joint, coin.

Exercise 15

1. shout	3. how	5. shock	7. spout	9. thaw
2. snow	4. growl	6. vouch	8. clean	10. ploy

Exercise 16

1. pound, town
2. frown, brown
3. street
4. haul
5. gown

6. cloud, mouth, trout
7. mow
8. must
9. snout
10. louse

Exercise 18

car column: 4, 5, 7
   for column: 3, 6, 10
   her column: 1, 2, 8, 9

Vowel Review

1. shaw
2. skaid
3. croy
4. blouk
5. brouch
6. cleet
7. prade
8. draze
9. baud
10. mube
11. chast
12. hok
13. gled
14. cust
15. nitch
16. flowt
17. shalk
18. slooch
19. cleak
20. pold

Answers to Pretests and Posttests

Pretest A

1. bloat	3. cloud	5. shout	7. shook	9. clown
2. creek	4. brawl	6. lawn	8. pool	10. fault

Pretest B

1. bare	3. sire	5. farm	7. cull	9. star
2. fir	4. purr	6. chalk	8. halt	10. fur

Pretest C

1. float, fleet, flout
2. dream
3. bleak
4. heel, howl, haul, heal, hail
5. shawl, shoal
6. bowl, bail, bawl, boil
7. clout, cleat
8. stain
9. stray, strow, straw
10. read, reed, rood, road, raid
11. shout, sheet, shoat, shoot
12. creak, creek, crook, croak
13. hoof
14. eel, ail, oil, awl, owl
15. three, throw
16. vault
17. threat, throat
18. bee, bay, boy, bow, boo
19. tool, tail, teal, toil
20. street, strait

Posttest A

1. clown	3. pool	5. breed	7. foil	9. croak
2. lean	4. sweet	6. broad	8. brown	10. spool

Posttest B

1. hear	3. shall	5. bear	7. chalk	9. mull
2. farm	4. call	6. care	8. short	10. pore

Posttest C

1. sweep, swoop
2. fault
3. scream
4. stray, straw
5. claim
6. towel
7. grouch
8. spoil, spool
9. blouse
10. joint, jaunt
11. flaunt
12. bray, brow
13. croak, crook, creak, creek
14. stay, stow
15. cloak
16. spray, spree
17. saint
18. shook
19. choose, chaise, cheese
20. preach

SUMMARY SHEET

Chapter 7

Record your scores for each test and exercise.

	Number Correct	**Instructor's Comments**
Pretest A	____out of 10 correct	
Pretest B	____out of 10 correct	
Pretest C	____out of 20 correct	
Exercise 1	____out of 24 correct	
Exercise 2	____out of 40 correct	
Exercise 3	____out of 10 correct	
Exercise 4	____out of 10 correct	
Exercise 5	____out of 10 correct	
Exercise 6	____out of 10 correct	
Exercise 7	____out of 10 correct	
Exercise 8	____out of 5 correct	
Exercise 9	____out of 5 correct	
Exercise 10	____out of 10 correct	
Exercise 11	____out of 12 correct	
Exercise 12	____out of 10 correct	
Exercise 13	____out of 15 correct	
Exercise 14	____out of 15 correct	
Exercise 15	____out of 10 correct	
Exercise 16	____out of 14 correct	
Exercise 17	____out of 10 correct	
Exercise 18	____out of 10 correct	
Vowel Review	____out of 20 correct	
Posttest A	____out of 10 correct	
Posttest B	____out of 10 correct	
Posttest C	____out of 20 correct	

8

Syllables

Glossary

Syllables: smaller parts or units of a word containing at least one vowel.

Compound Words: words that contain two or more smaller words, such as house/wife.

Base Words: small words that can stand alone.

Prefixes: word parts or syllables added to the beginning of a base word, as in *dis*/trust.

Suffixes: word parts or syllables added to the end of a base word, as in friend/*ly*.

Accent: the force or stress which you give to a syllable.

Schwa: the slurred sound of a vowel in an unaccented syllable.

Plural: a word that means more than one, as in boy—*boys*.

Entry Words: the bold printed words listed alphabetically in a dictionary.

Dictionary Respellings: the actual pronunciation of the entry words using dictionary symbols.

Stress: the force given to a syllable.

Homographs: pairs of words that are spelled the same but are pronounced differently.

Polysyllabic Words: words that have three or more syllables.

Introduction

In the chapters so far, you have learned about consonant and vowel sounds in small words. This chapter will bring these learnings together so that you can recognize and pronounce longer words.

Longer words can be broken down into smaller parts called *syllables.* Breaking a word into syllables helps you to sound out longer words.

In this chapter you will learn about *syllable patterns, compound words, open* and *closed syllables,* and silent *e* syllables. This chapter also discusses the *-le* pattern as well as *prefixes* and *suffixes.* Some dictionary skills, such as *accent marks, diacritical marks,* and the sound of the *schwa* make up the second part of the chapter.

Use Skilltape 8 to help you work through this chapter. The directions in this worktext will tell you when to turn on the skilltape.

The next section contains the pretests for Chapter 8. To see how much of the material in this chapter you already know, go now to Pretests A, B, and C. Complete each to the best of your ability.

P
R
E
T
E
S
T
S

Pretest A

Turn on Skilltape 8, side A.

Example: _3_

1. ____   6. ____

2. ____   7. ____

3. ____   8. ____

4. ____   9. ____

5. ____   10. ____

Pretest B

This pretest presents a list of words. Rewrite the words into syllables in the spaces provided.

Example: singing *sing-ing*

1. buckle _____   11. shameful _____

2. started _____   12. parked _____

3. maple _____   13. reporter _____

4. thousand _____   14. human _____

5. football _____   15. support _____

6. automobile _____   16. stressed _____

7. spider _____   17. simple _____

8. middle _____   18. campus _____

9. train _____   19. harmful _____

10. lemon _____   20. toiled _____

Pretest C

Look at the following words which have been divided into syllables. Pronounce each word to yourself and mark the accented syllable.

Example: demon de′-mon

1.	smother	smoth-er	6.	chuckle chuck-le
2.	athlete	ath-lete	7.	amazing a-maz-ing
3.	supper	sup-per	8.	intend in-tend
4.	allow	al-low	9.	strongest strong-est
5.	prefer	pre-fer	10.	misplace mis-place

Compare your answers to these pretests with those on page 206. Place a checkmark by each of your correct answers. Count the number correct for each pretest and write that number in the space provided here and on page 207.

> **Pretest A:** _____out of 10 correct
> **Pretest B:** _____out of 20 correct
> **Pretest C:** _____out of 10 correct
> **Total:** _____out of 40 correct

If you got 36 or more correct, you may go on to the posttests on pages 200–201. If you got less than 36 correct, complete this chapter and then take the posttests.

Two-syllable Words

In earlier chapters, all the words were small. Each word had only one vowel sound as in *car, steal,* and *side.* Words that have only one vowel sound are called *one-syllable words.* Longer words that have two vowel sounds are called *two-syllable words,* such as *outside, paper,* and *ribbon.* For every vowel sound you hear in a word, there is a syllable.

Part 1: Syllables

Exercise 1

Turn on the skilltape.

Key words: st<u>a</u>nd   ch<u>ea</u>t   br<u>a</u>k<u>e</u>
             d<u>e</u>m<u>o</u>n   c<u>o</u>lor   c<u>a</u>mp<u>u</u>s

Example: __2__

1. ___	6. ___	11. ___	16. ___
2. ___	7. ___	12. ___	17. ___
3. ___	8. ___	13. ___	18. ___
4. ___	9. ___	14. ___	19. ___
5. ___	10. ___	15. ___	20. ___

Record the number of correct answers here and on page 207.

Exercise 1:   ____out of 20 correct

Exercise 2

In this exercise, you will see many of the same words you just listened to on the tape. Underline all vowels and vowel combinations that you see in each word.

Examples: c<u>o</u>mp<u>e</u>t<u>e</u>   r<u>ea</u>d<u>i</u>ng

1. music
2. spider
3. beside
4. hundred
5. zipper

6. basketball
7. motorboat
8. magnet
9. trumpet
10. foolish

Turn on the skilltape.

Record the number of correct answers here and on page 207.

Exercise 2:   ____out of 23 correct

Compound Words

Many words in our language are made up of two or more smaller words. For example, *bedtime* and *bookcase* both have two smaller words in them—*bed* and *time*, *book* and *case*. We put them together, and they become words with more than one syllable.

You have learned that for each syllable there is one vowel sound. You have also learned that vowels which come between two consonants represent a short sound. *Bed* has a short *e* sound which is the only vowel sound in the word. *Bed* has one syllable. *Time* has a long *i* sound, because there is a final *e* which is silent. The long *i* is the only vowel you hear; therefore, *time* has one syllable. *Bedtime*, then, has two syllables.

Bookcase also has two syllables. In *book* there is one syllable, because there is only one vowel sound. *Case* has one syllable because it has one vowel sound. *Bookcase* has two syllables. Both *bedtime* and *bookcase* are called *compound words*.

> *Compound Words* are words that contain two or more smaller words. Example: *egg/shell*

Exercise 3

In this exercise, there are ten compound words. Draw a line between the two smaller words in each case. Pronounce the word to yourself. You should hear one vowel sound in each small word.

Example: egg/shell

1. flashlight
2. beefsteak
3. classroom
4. goldfish
5. cowboy

6. baseball
7. boxcar
8. eyebrow
9. lighthouse
10. earring

Compare your answers with those given on page 202. Place a checkmark by each of your correct answers. Count the number correct and record that number here and on page 207.

Exercise 3: _____ out of 10 correct

Exercise 4

Here is a list of small words. In the numbered spaces below, make compound words by using two of the smaller words. Pronounce the new word to yourself. You should hear one vowel sound in each small word.

hand	knob	sight	air
sea	stick	case	stand
mouse	plane	stair	top
tree	bow	lip	eye
food	trap	door	rain
girl	cow		

Example: *airplane*

1. _____   6. _____

2. _____   7. _____

3. _____   8. _____

4. _____   9. _____

5. _____   10. _____

Compare your answers with those given on page 202. Place a checkmark by each of your correct answers. Count the number correct and record that number here and on page 207.

Exercise 4: ____out of 10 correct

Prefixes and Suffixes

You have learned that compound words are made of two or more smaller words. These smaller words are sometimes referred to as *base words* because they can stand alone. In this section, you will learn how base words can be made longer by adding a word part called either a *prefix* or a *suffix*.

> A *prefix* is a word part or syllable added to the beginning of a base word. Example: <u>un</u>kind

> A *suffix* is a word part or syllable added to the end of a base word. Example: kind<u>ly</u>

Base words may contain both a prefix and suffix, as in *unfriendly*.

Table 1 presents two lists of the most common prefixes and suffixes. These common prefixes and suffixes are syllables. With your finger, cover the prefixes in each word and notice the base word. Do the same with the suffixes. Recognizing familiar prefixes and suffixes will help you to pronounce longer words that you don't know.

Table 1

Common Prefixes and Suffixes

Prefixes	*Suffixes*
in- (as in *inside*)	-er (as in *player*)
un- (as in *unhook*)	-ing (as in *singing*)
mis- (as in *misfire*)	-ness (as in *goodness*)
de- (as in *deport*)	-ish (as in *foolish*)
re- (as in *regain*)	-ly (as in *slowly*)
dis- (as in *disorder*)	-hood (as in *childhood*)
for- (as in *forget*)	-less (as in *homeless*)
fore- (as in *foreground*)	-ful (as in *careful*)
	-en (as in *wooden*)
	-est (as in *hardest*)

Exercise 5

Each of the words in this exercise contains either a common prefix or suffix. Some words may have both. First, circle the base word. Then, underline the prefix or suffix. Then pronounce each word to yourself.

Example: dis(like)

1. untie
2. recover
3. display
4. kindness
5. manhood

6. depart
7. inside
8. nicely
9. foolish
10. louder

Compare your answers with those given on page 202. Place a checkmark by each part of your correct answer (each number has two parts). Count the number correct and record that number here and on page 207.

Exercise 5: _____ out of 20 correct

Exercise 6

un-	-ful	-est
dis-	-less	-ly
re-	-er	-en

Add one of the above prefixes or suffixes to the base in each the the following sentences which best completes the sentence. You may use a prefix or suffix more than once. Write the new word in the space provided.

Example: The crowd at the baseball game thought the umpire was (prefix)fair. _*unfair*_

1. I (prefix)agree with the teacher's plan for an outing. _____

2. Did you know that dancers are grace(suffix)? _____

3. Jane was asked to (prefix)fill the candy dish. _____

4. The Concorde flew swift(suffix) across the ocean. _____

5. Some people say that Muhammad Ali is the great(suffix) heavyweight boxer of all time. _____

6. The help(suffix) rabbit was caught by the hunter's trap. _____

7. The child was asked to (prefix)lock the door so his parents could get in. _____

8. When the leaves fall to the ground, the garden(suffix) will rake them. _____

9. On the Fourth of July there is always a (prefix)play of fireworks in the park. _____

10. Sugar is used to sweet(suffix) some drinks. _____

Compare your answers with those given on page 202. Place a checkmark by each of your correct answers. Count the number correct and record that number here and on page 207.

Exercise 6:   ____out of 10 correct

The Ending -ED

Exercise 7

Look at these words: *started, stopped squealed.*

Turn on the skilltape.

Example: lasted   _2_ *ed*

1. bonded ____ ____
2. walked ____ ____
3. sharpened ____ ____
4. hounded ____ ____
5. flaked ____ ____

6. buttoned ____ ____
7. tested ____ ____
8. traveled ____ ____
9. kissed ____ ____
10. piloted ____ ____

Compare your answers with those on page 202. Place a checkmark by each part of your correct answers (each number has two parts). Count the number correct and record that number here and on page 207.

Exercise 7:   ____out of 20 correct

The Sound of -ED

Look at the following words:

land	landed
plant	planted
part	parted
intend	intended
test	tested

The base words in the first column end in *d* or *t*. When *-ed* is added to a base word ending in *d* or *t*, as illustrated in the second column, you pronounce the *ed* as a separate syllable.

Generally, after any other letter, the suffix *-ed* is pronounced as a *d* or *t* and is not a separate syllable. Examples: *smiled, stabbed, walked, talked.* Each of these words has only one syllable because you hear only one vowel sound. In the word *attacked,* you hear two syllables—*at/tacked. Ashamed* also has two syllables—*a/ shamed.*

Exercise 8

Making use of the clues you have just learned, decide on how many syllables there are in each of the following words. Write the number of syllables in the space provided.

Example: seated _2_   fixed _1_

1. treated_____
2. stopped_____
3. played_____
4. bloated_____
5. looked_____

6. ended_____
7. loaned_____
8. missed_____
9. parted_____
10. phoned_____

Compare your answers with those given on page 202. Place a checkmark by each of your correct answers. Count the number correct and record that number here and on page 207.

Exercise 8:   _____out of 10 correct

The Suffixes -ER, -EST, -ED, -ING

When you break a word down to help in pronouncing it, you remove the suffix in order to be able to recognize the base word. The form of the base word often changes when the suffixes *-er, -est, -ed,* and *-ing* are added to it. The following exercises will help you to recognize base words that have these suffixes.

Exercise 9

Samples: hitter = hitt́ − er = hit
          stopping = stopṕ − ing = stop

Using the samples above, break down the following words. Pronounce the base word to yourself without the suffix, using your knowledge of vowels. Then pronounce it with the suffix.

Example: thinner *thinn er*

1. swimming   _____ _____
2. shopped   _____ _____
3. wrapping   _____ _____
4. planner   _____ _____

5. dropping ___ ___

6. runner ___ ___

7. snapped ___ ___

8. fattest ___ ___

9. scrapping ___ ___

10. thinnest ___ ___

Compare your answers with those given on page 202. Place a checkmark by each part of your correct answers (each number has two parts). Count the number correct and record that number here and on page 207.

Exercise 9: ___out of 20 correct

Exercise 10

Samples: *dealer = deal + er*
  speeding = speed + ing
  sticking = stick + ing
  shortest = short + est

Using the samples above, break down the following words. Pronounce the base word to yourself. Then pronounce it with the suffix.

Examples: *scolded*   *scold ed*
  speaker   *speak er*

1. coldest ___ ___

2. greater ___ ___

3. standing ___ ___

4. darkest ___ ___

5. greeting ___ ___

6. beaded ___ ___

7. looped ___ ___

8. harder ___ ___

9. herded ___ ___

10. sweetest ___ ___

Compare your answers with those given on page 202. Place a checkmark by each part of your correct answers (each number has two parts). Count the number correct and record that number here and on page 207.

Exercises 10: ___out of 20 correct

Exercise 11

Sample: waving = wave + ing

Using the sample above, break down the following words. Pronounce the base word to yourself. Then pronounce it with the suffix.

Example: taping *tape* *ing*

1. filing   ____ ____
2. wasted   ____ ____
3. skater   ____ ____
4. tasted   ____ ____
5. driving   ____ ____
6. bravest   ____ ____
7. riding   ____ ____
8. skating   ____ ____
9. finest   ____ ____
10. joker   ____ ____

Compare your answers with those given on page 202. Place a checkmark by each part of your correct answers (each number has two parts). Count the number correct and record that number here and on page 207.

Exercise 11:   ____out of 20 correct

Review Exercise 1

Turn on the skilltape.

Example: reported _3_

1. disagreed____   4. misspelled____
2. kissed____   5. designing____
3. repeat____   6. unspoken____

7. forbidden____   11. signed____

8. boating____   12. manhood____

9. forecast____   13. fearless____

10. careful____   14. fondness____

Record the number of correct answers here and on page 207.

Review Exercise 1: ____out of 44 correct

Review Exercise 2

For each of the words in this exercise, draw a line through any vowel that is not heard in the word. As you have learned, there are reasons why vowels are not sounded. Apply these principles to this exercise. Then count the number of syllables and place that number in the space provided.

Example: disbarrӨd _2_

1. repressed____   6. inside____

2. displease____   7. misfire____

3. homeless____   8. regain____

4. derail____   9. fairest____

5. unseeming____   10. treated____

Compare your answers with those given on page 203. Place a checkmark by each part of your correct answers (each number has several parts). Count the number correct and record that number here and on page 207.

Review Exercise 2: ____out of 21 correct

Review Exercise 3

Look at each word in this exercise. If there is a prefix, write it in the column headed *prefix*. Write the base word in the second column. A base word must be a complete word. If the final *e* had been removed from the base word, replace it; if the final consonant of the base word had been doubled, drop the second consonant. Then write any suffix in the third column.

		Prefix	*Base Word*	*Suffix*
Example:	unfriendly	*un*	*friend*	*ly*
1.	refreshing	re	fresh	ing
2.	misspelled	mis	spelled	
3.	mistaken	mis	tak	en
4.	reshaped	re	shaped	
5.	painless		pain	less
6.	dismissed	dis	missed	
7.	replaced	re	placed	
8.	departed	de	part	ed
9.	tapping		tap	ping
10.	unfeeling	un	feel	ing
11.	dismounted	dis	mount	ed
12.	freshness			
13.	freshest			
14.	distasteful			
15.	forgotten			
16.	swifter			
17.	unchanging			
18.	misprinted			
19.	thankless			
20.	retrained			

Compare your answers with those given on page 203. Place a checkmark by each part of your correct answer (each syllable). Count the number correct and record it here and on page 207.

Review Exercise 3: _____ **out of 54 correct**

Patterns for Breaking It Down

The previous exercises have shown you how words are broken down by removing prefixes and suffixes and breaking compound words into smaller words. This section discusses how to break down longer words which do not have suffixes and prefixes and are not compound words.

There are several patterns that help in breaking words down into syllables. These patterns are only aids to pronunciation. The patterns will help you to view a longer word in smaller parts which are easier to pronounce.

Vowel-Consonant-Consonant-Vowel Pattern

One of the easiest patterns to understand is the vowel-consonant-consonant-vowel or *VCCV* pattern. In this pattern, we break a word down by looking for two consonants together. If a vowel sound is found before and after the two consonants, then you divide the word between the two consonants. Examples: sum/mit, win/dow.

Exercise 12

Using the 'VCCV' pattern, rewrite each of the following words in the spaces provided.

Example: happen *hap/pen*

1. batter ____ / ____
2. cannon ____ / ____
3. picnic ____ / ____
4. selfish ____ / ____
5. suspect ____ / ____

6. ladder ____ / ____
7. harbor ____ / ____
8. cinder ____ / ____
9. supper ____ / ____
10. goblet ____ / ____

Compare your answers with those on page 203. Place a checkmark by each correct part of your answer (each syllable). Count the number correct and record that number here and on page 207.

Exercise 12: ____ out of 20 correct

Accented Syllables

Look at these words: *magnet, hammer, ribbon.* In these words, the first vowel is followed by two consonants. The first syllable ends with the first consonant—mag/net, ham/mer, rib/bon. You have already learned that in small words a vowel is short when it is the only vowel in the word and it is immediately followed by a consonant (*at, bat, stag, shack*). This same rule applies to syllables which are *accented.* Many words with two syllables are accented on the first syllable.

> *Accent* is the force or stress which you give to a syllable.

Turn on Skilltape 8, side B.

Exercise 13

Samples: taś/səl   siś/tər   blań/kət

Example: _short i_

1. _____   6. _____
2. _____   7. _____
3. _____   8. _____
4. _____   9. _____
5. _____   10. _____

Record the number of correct answers here and on page 207.

Exercise 13:   _____out of 10 correct

Review Exercise 4

Using previous information from this book, break the following words into syllables. Look for any prefixes and suffixes in words, compound words, and words that follow the *VCCV* pattern. Pronounce each word carefully to yourself. Some words may have only one syllable. If so, leave it alone.

Example: fireplace *fire, place*

1. sister ____/____
2. doorknob ____/____
3. hammer ____/____
4. meaning ____/____
5. perhaps ____/____
6. cancel ____/____
7. enter ____/____
8. parted ____/____
9. shopped ____/____
10. remark ____/____
11. forecast ____/____
12. depart ____/____
13. darkness ____/____
14. pillow ____/____
15. starter ____/____
16. oatmeal ____/____
17. stoned ____/____
18. peanut ____/____
19. wisdom ____/____
20. misspelled ____/____

Compare your answers with those on page 203. Place a checkmark by each part of your correct answer (each syllable). Count the number correct and record that number here and on page 207.

Review Exercise 4: ____out of 38 correct

Turn on the skilltape.

Vowel-Consonant-Vowel Pattern

A second pattern for breaking down words is the vowel-consonant-vowel pattern (*VCV*). Generally, when one consonant follows the first vowel, you divide the word before that consonant. Examples: cri/sis (v/cv), stu/dent (v/cv).

Notice that in these examples, the vowel comes at the end of the first syllable. You will remember that one of the rules for vowel sounds in small words was: "when a vowel comes at the end of a word, the vowel sound is long" (*she, be, go*). This same rule applies to *syllables* in longer words (*lo/cust, pre/vent*).

Now look at the words *never, tragic, comic.* If you were to divide these words according to the *VCV* pattern (that is, divide the word after the first vowel) and then apply your knowledge of vowels, the vowel sound in the first syllable would be long. Pronounce the words in this way: *ne/ver, tra/gic, co/mic.* Do they sound like words you know? No, they do not.

If, after using the vowel-consonant-vowel pattern, the word is not familiar, then divide the words *after* the consonant: *nev/er, trag/ic, com/ic*. Remember that when a vowel comes in the middle of a word or syllable, the vowel sound is short. Can you pronounce these words correctly now?

In *never,* the vowel sound in the first syllable is short because it is the only vowel and it comes in the middle of the syllable. In the second syllable, the *e* is slurred and represents the *schwa* sound.

> A *schwa* represents the slurred sound of a vowel in an unaccented syllable.

This sound will be discussed in more detail later in this chapter.

In *tragic,* the vowel sound in the first syllable is a short *a* and the *i* in the second syllable represents a short *i* sound. The *g* in the first syllable represents a *j* sound, as in *gin.* Remember that in most cases *g* followed by *e, i,* or *y* represents a *j* sound. The final *c* represents a *k* sound. When *c* is *not* followed by *e, i,* or *y,* it represents a *k* sound.

The vowel sound in the first syllable in *comic* represents a short *o.* The vowel sound in the second syllable represents a short *i* sound. Both *c*'s represent a *k* sound.

Exercise 14

Turn on the skilltape.

Example: metal *met/ al*

1. petal ____/____	6. token ____/____
2. miser ____/____	7. visit ____/____
3. frozen ____/____	8. labor ____/____
4. linen ____/____	9. recent ____/____
5. human ____/____	10. driven ____/____

Turn on the skilltape.

Record the number of correct answers here and on page 207.

Record the number of correct answers here and on page 207.

Exercise 14:   ____out of 20 correct

The -LE Pattern

Look at the following words: *gen/tle, cra/dle.* In these words, the last syllable ends in *-le.* The consonant before the *-le* begins the last syllable.

Notice that in the word *gen/tle* there is one vowel in the first syllable, and it comes in the middle. It represents a short *e* sound. The *g* represents the *j* sound because it comes before the *e.* In *cra/dle* there is one vowel, and it comes at the end of the first syllable. It represents a long *a* sound. The *c* represents a *k* sound because it is followed by a letter other than *e, i, y.*

Note: When there is a *-ck* before *le,* as in *buckle,* divide the syllable after the *k* (*buck/le*).

Exercise 15

Divide the following words into syllables.

Example: ladle *la͜ dle*

1. crackle ___ / ___
2. handle ___ / ___
3. scramble ___ / ___
4. puddle ___ / ___
5. trickle ___ / ___

6. thimble ___ / ___
7. bible ___ / ___
8. fable ___ / ___
9. title ___ / ___
10. speckle ___ / ___

Compare your answers with those given on page 203. Place a checkmark by each part of your correct answer (each syllable). Count the number correct and record that number here and on page 207.

Exercise 15: ___ **out of 20 correct**

Consonant Blends and Digraphs in Syllables

Look at the following words: *a/pron, moth/er.* In *apron* there is a *pr* blend. In *mother* there is a *th* digraph. Blends and digraphs are not usually separated when a word is broken into syllables.

When you see a blend or digraph in a word, consider it as one consonant as you break the word into syllables. Examples: *re/spect, far/ther.*

Exercise 16

Divide the following words into syllables.

Example: tether *teth / er*

1. hundred ___ / ___
2. zebra ___ / ___
3. bushel ___ / ___
4. monster ___ / ___
5. portray ___ / ___

6. orchard ___ / ___
7. contract ___ / ___
8. secret ___ / ___
9. other ___ / ___
10. smother ___ / ___

Compare your answers with those given on page 203. Place a checkmark by each part of your correct answer (each syllable). Count the number correct and record that number here and on page 207.

Exercise 16: ___out of 20 correct

Vowel Combinations in Syllables

Another consideration when breaking words down is vowel combinations. Generally, vowel digraphs (*ea, ee, ie, ei, ai, ay, au, aw*) are not divided. Also, vowel diphthongs (*ou, ow, oi, oy*) are not divided.

When considering which pattern to use in breaking words down, you treat vowel combinations as if they are one vowel. For instance, *moun/tain* has a *VCCV* pattern. The *ou* and *ai* are each considered one vowel and the word is divided between the consonants.

In *ap/point* you divide between the two consonants because there is also a *VCCV* pattern. The *oi* in the second syllable is considered one vowel.

Au/thor has a *V/CV* pattern. The *au* in the first syllable is treated as one vowel. The *th* is a consonant digraph which is not separated.

When words with a silent *e*, such as *re/place* and *ad/vise* are broken down, the syllable with the silent *e* should be treated as a small word. The rule, you remember, is: "When silent *e* is at the end of a word, the previous vowel is usually long."

Review Exercise 5

Using all you have learned so far, divide the following words into syllables. Look for smaller words in compound words, prefixes and suffixes, and -*le*. Also look for *VCCV* and *VCV* patterns.

Example: repeat   *re peat*

1. grocer ____/____
2. precook ____/____
3. spotted ____/____
4. cheerful ____/____
5. eyesight ____/____
6. hopeless ____/____
7. master ____/____
8. student ____/____
9. river ____/____
10. rotate ____/____
11. reread ____/____
12. punish ____/____
13. speckle ____/____
14. counted ____/____
15. scramble ____/____
16. neatness ____/____
17. moisture ____/____
18. handsome ____/____
19. oatmeal ____/____
20. unfair ____/____

Compare your answers with those given on page 204. Place a checkmark by each part (each syllable) of your correct answer. Count the number correct and record that number here and on page 207.

Review Exercise 5:   ____out of 40 correct

Sounds of Y

There are four sounds of *y* in our language. You have learned that when *y* is the first letter in a word, it is a consonant, as in *yes, yet,* and *yard.* You have also learned that *y* may be a vowel when it comes at the end of small words and has the sound of long *i,* as in *why, my,* and *cry.* When these small words are found in two- (or more) syllable words, such as *crying, drying,* and *butterfly,* the *y* continues to have the long *i* sound.

In other words of two or more syllables, the *y* may represent a long *e* sound—as in *puppy, merry,* and *daisy*—or a long *i* sound—as in *rely, reply,* and *satisfy.*

Exercise 17

Turn on the skilltape.

Example: fly _ı̇_

1. cycle____
2. pretty____
3. tiny____
4. deny____
5. baby____

6. happy____
7. supply____
8. dry____
9. crying____
10. merry____

Compare your answers with those given on page 204. Place a checkmark by each correct answer. Count the number correct and record that number here and on page 207.

Exercise 17: ____out of 10 correct

Other Rules for the Sound of Y

Y may also sound like a short *i*, as in *gypsy, gym, gymnast,* and *cyst.* The letter *y* may represent a short *i* sound when it is the only vowel in the middle of a small word or syllable. In the following words, the *y* has a short *i* sound:

gym	gypsy
mystic	system
cyst	symbol

Words ending in *ey* have the long *e* sound, as in *money, honey, monkey,* and *donkey.*

Exercise 18

Break the following words into syllables. Decide which sound of *y* you hear. Write *e* or *i* in the boxes provided.

Example: freely *free/ly* ☐ e

1. kindly ____/____ ☐
2. witty ____/____ ☐
3. gravy ____/____ ☐
4. flying ____/____ ☐
5. daily ____/____ ☐

6. reply ____/____ ☐
7. supply ____/____ ☐
8. lately ____/____ ☐
9. twenty ____/____ ☐
10. fifty ____/____ ☐

Compare your answers with those given on page 204. Place a checkmark by each part (each syllable and box) of your correct answers. Count your correct answers and record that number here and on page 207.

Exercise 18: _____out of 30 correct

Endings

Look at the following words: *hands, dishes, babies.* Notice that these words end in -*s*, -*es*, and -*ies*. These endings are plural forms. What base word do you see in *hands?* In *dishes?* In *babies?* The base words are *hand, dish,* and *baby.* -*S* was added to *hand* to make the plural form *hands,* -*es* was added to *dish* to make the plural form *dishes.* However, in the word *baby,* it was necessary to change the *y* to *i* and then add -*es.*

> *Plural* means more than
> one. Examples — I have
> *one* bat. I have *three* bats.

Exercise 19

Write the base word of the following plural forms.

Example: dresses ___*dress*___

1. taxes_____
2. rabbits_____
3. parties_____
4. crosses_____
5. glasses_____

6. candies_____
7. brushes_____
8. camels_____
9. belts_____
10. pennies_____

Compare your answers with those given on page 204. Place a checkmark by each of your correct answers. Count the number correct and record that number here and on page 207.

Exercise 19: _____out of 10 correct

A General Rule for Plural Syllables

Generally, in words which have -*es* (or -*ies*) in their plural form, the -*es* and -*ies* make a separate syllable.

Exercise 20

Divide the following plural words into syllables. If there is only one syllable, leave it alone.

Example   buddies   *bud/dies*

1. bodies ____/____
2. inches ____/____
3. copies ____/____
4. frogs ____/____
5. speeches ____/____

6. armies ____/____
7. marries ____/____
8. witches ____/____
9. coaches ____/____
10. girls ____/____

Compare your answers to those given on page 204. Place a checkmark by each syllable of your correct answer: Count the number correct and record that number here and on page 207.

Exercise 20:   ____out of 18 correct

Part II: Dictionary Skills

You have learned how to break words down by recognizing compound words, common prefixes and suffixes, common base words, and patterns in words. After breaking words into syllables, you were able to apply phonic principles that you learned earlier in this worktext so that you could pronounce each syllable and the whole word. There are times, however, when after breaking down the word and applying phonic rules you may not recognize the word because you have never heard it before. Other times, you will not be able to pronounce the word because phonic rules do not seem to work. When this occurs, you need to refer to a dictionary. In this part of the chapter, you will learn some basic skills to help you use a dictionary:

1. diacritical marks: *hate* (hāt), *hat* (hăt)
2. Accent marks: *repeat* (ri/pet′)
3. Schwa: *about* (ə/bout)

Diacritical Marks

Diacritical marks are marks that are used in dictionaries to show the sound of a letter, usually a vowel. The two most common marks are the macron (–) and the breve (˘). The macron is used to indicate a long vowel sound. The breve is used to indicate a short vowel sound. Many dictionaries use these marks. However, different dictionaries may use a variety of marks and symbols to help you pronounce words. At the end of this section, we will discuss other marks and symbols.

Exercise 21

Say each of the following words to yourself; then mark the vowel sounds. Place a macron (–) over the vowel if the vowel is long. If the vowel is short, use a breve (˘). If the vowel is silent, cross it out.

Examples: māke̸   fı̆t

1. stove	6. loaf
2. end	7. speed
3. glad	8. shock
4. wife	9. brunt
5. man	10. mute

Compare your answers with those given on page 204. Place a checkmark by each correct mark in your answers. Count the number correct and record that number here and on page 207.

Exercise 21: _____**out of 15 correct**

Exercise 22

Turn on the skilltape.

Examples: ā̲ ŏ̲

1. ____   6. ____

2. ____   7. ____

3. ____   8. ____

4. ____   9. ____

5. ____   10. ____

Compare your answers with those given on page 204. Place a checkmark by each of your correct answers. Count the number correct and record that number here and on page 207.

Exercise 22: ____out of 10 correct

The Schwa Sound

In words that have two or more syllables, one of the syllable may not have a long or short vowel sound or any other recognizable, distinct vowel sound. The vowel sound that you hear may be slurred. This slurred vowel sound is called *schwa*. Any vowel (*a,e,i,o,u*) may have the *schwa* sound. The symbol for the *schwa* in many dictionaries is an inverted or upside down *e* (ə). Look at the following word: *alone*. Say the word to yourself. In the first syllable, there is the vowel *a*. It is neither long nor short. This vowel has the *schwa* sound. In a dictionary, the word might look like this for pronunciation purposes: *a/lone* (ə lōn).

When you use a dictionary to pronounce an unknown word, you will find that word first in boldface print. This is called an *entry* word. It is often divided into syllables.

> *Entry words* are the boldface printed words listed alphabetically in a dictionary.

Following the entry word is the dictionary respelling of that word which uses the diacritical marks you have learned in this chapter. It is in this respelling that you will find the symbol for the *schwa*. Examples: **va/cant** (vā kənt); **so/da** (sō də).

Exercise 23

In the following exercise, there are five words on the left with dictionary respellings. Find the word in Column B that matches the word in Column A, and write it in the space.

Column A	*Column B*	
Example: pilet *pilot*		
1. kō me_____	comma	metal
2. kăb en_____	robin	coma
3. měd el_____	medal	cabin
4. mi̇ nes_____	minus	carbon
5. rŏb en_____	menace	robber
	pillow	pilot

Compare your answers with those given on page 204. Place a checkmark by each of your correct answers. Count the number correct and record that number here and on page 207.

Exercise 23: _____out of 5 correct

Turn on the skilltape.

Dictionary Respellings

Examples: vital (vī təl)
concise (kən sīs)
conceal (kən sēl)
color (kŭl ər)
banana (bə năn ə)

> *Dictionary respellings* do not have silent consonants or vowels and use only the letters that represent the actual sound. Words are respelled exactly as they sound.

Accents

In words with two or more syllables, there are differences in the way each syllable may be stressed when you say the word. One syllable will have more stress than another.

> *Stress* is the force given to a syllable.

The way syllables are stressed is called *accent*. An accent mark (') is used to show the syllable which has the *most* stress or force. This is called the *primary accent*. When words have three or four syllables, there may be two accented syllables. One is *primary* and the other is *secondary*. The secondary accent is represented by a lighter mark. Some dictionaries place the accent mark before the syllable; others, after the syllable. Clues to accents are complicated and inconsistent. Therefore, use a dictionary to determine the stress given to syllables.

Exercise 24

The following words have been divided into syllables. Pronounce each word to yourself and place an accent mark after the syllable that is stressed. You may wish to consult a dictionary.

Example: mem'/ber

1. ap/ple
2. pic/ture
3. kit/ten
4. ta/ble
5. a/way

6. emp/ty
7. den/tist
8. win/dow
9. per/haps
10. po/lite

Compare your answers with those given on page 204. Place a checkmark by each correct mark. Count the number correct and record that number here and on page 207.

Exercise 24:   _____out of 10 correct

Accent and Vowel Sounds

It is the accent in a word that makes vowels have *clear* short and long sounds. In unaccented syllables, the vowel sounds are usually slurred and have the schwa sound. Look at this word: *commute* (kə mūt'). Can you pronounce it? The first syllable is unaccented and has the schwa sound; whereas, the second syllable is accented and has a *clear* long *u* sound. In the word *bottom* (bot′ əm), the first (accented) syllable has a short *o* sound, but the *o* in the unaccented syllable has a schwa sound.

Homographs

There are several pairs of words that, although spelled the same, are pronounced differently. These words are called *homographs*. Look at the following words and notice how they are used in the sample sentences:

record   I bought a new *record*. (rĕk′ ərd)
            I will *record* my voice on tape. (ri kord′)

present   She got a *present* for her birthday. (prĕz′ ənt)
            He will *present* a medal to the soldier. (pri zĕnt′)

content   The dog was *content* after eating. (kən tĕnt′)
            The *content* of the history course was difficult. (kŏn′ tĕnt)

Each of the above words is spelled the same, but pronounced differently, depending on the sentence or context in which it is used. When you read a sentence that contains a homograph and you are familiar with the context, you will be able to pronounce the word. However, if the word is unfamiliar to you, you must use a dictionary to determine the correct pronunciation.

Exercise 25

Turn on the skilltape.

Example: re/ply′ ⌣⌣

1. a/muse____
2. met/al____
3. pa/rade____
4. stan/za____
5. cli/mate____

6. co/bra____
7. pitch/er____
8. bee/tle____
9. bot/tle____
10. e/vade____

Compare your answers with those given on page 204. Place a checkmark by each part of your correct answers (each word has two parts). Count the number correct and record that number here and on page 207.

Exercise 25: ____out of 20 correct

Polysyllable Words

Words which have three or more syllables are called *polysyllable words*. To break down polysyllable words, the procedures are basically the same as breaking down two-syllable words. Remember:

> *Poly* is a prefix meaning "many." *Polysyllable words* are words which have three or more syllables.

1. Look for compound words.
2. Look for prefixes, suffixes, and base words.
3. Count the number of vowels in the word that can be heard. This will tell how many syllables are in the word.
4. Use the patterns *VC/CV*, *V/CV*, *VC/V*, and *-le* when possible.
5. Then pronounce each syllable by using phonic rules which you have learned. Blend the syllables together and say the word.
6. When patterns do not work, use a dictionary.

Exercise 26

Look at the following compound words. Break them down using patterns where possible to help you.

Example: grandfather *grand/fa/ther*

1. superman_____
2. grandmother_____
3. blackberry_____
4. evergreen_____
5. basketball_____

6. candlelight_____
7. loudspeaker_____
8. drillmaster_____
9. gentleman_____
10. marketplace_____

Compare your answers with those given on page 205. Place a checkmark, by the number of each correct answer. Count the number correct and record that number here and on page 207.

Exercise 26:   ___out of 10 correct

Recognizable Components

There are prefixes, suffixes, and other parts of words which appear again and again. These are spelled the same and almost always are pronounced the same. They usually appear before or after familiar base words and are generally syllables in themselves. Tables 2, 3, and 4 offer lists of these recognizable components with examples.

Table 2

Prefixes

con	*con*tract	*con*sume	*con*form
per	*per*haps	*per*cent	*per*sist
pre	*pre*fer	*pre*dict	*pre*cise
pro	*pro*cede	*pro*vide	*pro*duce
trans	*trans*port	*trans*fer	*trans*istor
sub	*sub*marine	*sub*heading	*sub*tract
inter	*inter*fere	*inter*ject	*inter*lock
ex	*ex*cuse	*ex*tra	*ex*tend

Table 3

Suffixes

-ed	test*ed*	hunt*ed*	jail*ed*
-able (əb əl)	pass*able*	belie*vable**	lo*vable**
-ment	parch*ment*	state*ment*	pay*ment*
-al (el)	comic*al*	termin*al*	person*al*
-ible (əb əl)	poss*ible*	permiss*ible*	sens*ible*

*Remember, when a suffix begins with a vowel and the base word ends in a silent *e*, the *e* is dropped before the suffix.

Table 4

More Recognizable Components

-ive (ĭv)	*-age* (ĭj)	*-ate* (āt)	*-ate* (ĭt)	*-ine* (ēn)
adject*ive*	bagg*age*	imit*ate*	delic*ate*	mar*ine*
posit*ive*	lugg*age*	elev*ate*	priv*ate*	gasol*ine*
pass*ive*	garb*age*	separ*ate*	sen*ate*	magaz*ine*
permiss*ive*	cott*age*			
intens*ive*	im*age*			

-ine (ĭn)	*-ous* (ŭs)
eng*ine*	joy*ous*
medic*ine*	humor*ous*
margar*ine*	danger*ous*
	glori*ous*

Look at the following words: *nation, social,* and *mission.* In these words, the letter combinations of *ti, ci,* and *si* sound like *sh.* Table 5 illustrates this combination with some recognizable components.

Table 5

-TI, -CI, and -SI

-sion (zhən)	*-sion* (shən)	*-tion* (shən)	*-tial* (shəl)
divi*sion*	expres*sion*	na*tion*	par*tial*
inva*sion*	transmis*sion*	ac*tion*	spa*tial*
televi*sion*	posses*sion*	posi*tion*	essen*tial*

-ture (chər)	*-cial* (shəl)	*-cian* (shən)	*-cious* (shəs)
na*ture*	spe*cial*	musi*cian*	vi*cious*
pic*ture*	so*cial*	physi*cian*	deli*cious*
lec*ture*	ra*cial*	electri*cian*	pre*cious*

-ic (ĭk)

electr*ic*

atom*ic*

com*ic*

Exercise 27

Break down the following polysyllabic words.

Example: reloading *re/load/ing*

1. truthfulness_____
2. usefulness_____
3. watchfully_____
4. playfulness_____
5. refillable_____
6. construction_____
7. washable_____
8. preheated_____
9. unfairly_____

10. unlikely_____

11. transportable_____

12. excitement_____

13. disagreement_____

14. subhuman_____

15. production_____

16. protective_____

17. interaction_____

18. prediction_____

19. transfusion_____

20. respectable_____

Compare your answers with those given on page 205. Place a checkmark by the number of each correct answer. Count the number correct and record that number here and on page 207.

Exercise 27: ____out of 20 correct

Exercise 28

Break down the following polysyllabic words.

1. artificial_____

2. substantial_____

3. sensitive_____

4. breakage_____

5. confidential_____

6. constitution_____

7. disgraceful_____

8. inexpertly_____

9. disagreeable_____

10. baggage_____

11. inadvisable_____

12. industrious_____

13. departure_____

14. conclusion_____

15. transferable_____

16. nicotine_____

17. adequate_____

18. delicious_____

19. athletic_____

20. exotic_____

Compare your answers with those given on page 205. Place a checkmark by the number of each correct answer. Count the number correct and record that number here and on page 207.

Exercise 28: _____out of 20 correct

Exercise 29

Part A

In the following words, count the vowel sounds you hear. Remember, do not count final *e* (it is probably silent). When two vowels are together, count them as one sound. Do not count the *u* after *q*.

Example: entertained __3__

1. magazine____
2. oculist____
3. wilderness____
4. afforded____
5. trumpeted____

6. revealing____
7. compound____
8. knuckle____
9. equipped____
10. acquainted____

Part B

Now that you know how many syllables there are, use your knowledge of patterns to break the word down.

Example: entertained *en/ter/tained*

1. magazine_____
2. oculist_____
3. wilderness_____
4. afforded_____
5. trumpeted_____

6. revealing_____
7. compound_____
8. knuckle_____
9. equipped_____
10. acquainted_____

Compare your answers to the two parts of this exercise to those given on page 205. Place a checkmark by the number of each correct answer. Count the number correct and record that number here and on page 207.

Exercise 29, Part A: ____out of 10 correct
Part B: ____out of 10 correct

Dictionary Symbols

If you have tried to pronounce a word using the phonic generalizations and rules of syllabication and still cannot, then consult a dictionary.

After each entry word in a dictionary, you will find the pronunciation or dictionary respelling of that word. Each symbol found in the dictionary respelling stands for one sound. Look at the following examples: *weigh* (wā). For this word, the dictionary respelling shows a long *a* sound, because the letters *eigh* have the long *a* sound. In the word *scale* (skāl), the dictionary respelling shows the *s* followed by a *k* sound and a long *a*. The *e* is not shown because it is silent.

Most dictionaries will use approximately 40 different symbols to represent 40 different sounds. Table 6 on page 198 is a typical pronunciation key which might be found in a dictionary.

Table 6

Pronunciation Key

b	<u>b</u>at	ă	<u>a</u>t
d	<u>d</u>og	ā	<u>a</u>te
f	<u>f</u>un	ã (â)	c<u>a</u>re
g	<u>g</u>un	ä	f<u>a</u>r
h	<u>h</u>at	ĕ	p<u>e</u>t
j	<u>j</u>og	ē	m<u>ea</u>t
k	<u>k</u>ing	ĭ	p<u>i</u>n
l	<u>l</u>amp	ī	p<u>i</u>ne
m	<u>m</u>ap	ŏ	h<u>o</u>t
n	<u>n</u>ap	ō	h<u>o</u>pe
p	<u>p</u>an	ô	l<u>aw</u>
r	<u>r</u>an	ŭ	g<u>u</u>n
s	<u>s</u>at	o͞o	m<u>oo</u>n
t	<u>t</u>an	yo͞o	f<u>ew</u>
v	<u>v</u>an	er	b<u>ir</u>d, b<u>ur</u>n
w	<u>w</u>in	ə	<u>a</u>mount
y	<u>y</u>es	o͝o	c<u>oo</u>k or
z	<u>z</u>oo	u	f<u>u</u>ll
		oi	<u>oi</u>l, t<u>o</u>y
		ou	<u>ou</u>t, <u>ow</u>l
		ch	<u>ch</u>in
		sh	<u>sh</u>oe
		ng	si<u>ng</u>
		th	<u>th</u>in
		th	<u>th</u>is
		zh	mea<u>s</u>ure
		ū	f<u>u</u>me

Exercise 30

The following words are spelled as they would be in a dictionary using dictionary symbols. Pronounce these words to your instructor.

Example: (ek sĕpt′) except

1. (păl ĭs)
2. (ĕg zăkt′)
3. (bŭj ĭt)
4. (dĭ vī′ siv)
5. (ji ra shən)

6. (măn′ dāt)
7. (kwôr′ əm)
8. (spăch ə lə)
9. (to͞oz′ dā)
10. (vĕr′ ə fī)

Record the number of correct answers here and on page 207.

Exercise 30: _____out of 10 correct

Exercise 31

The following entry words can be found in a dictionary. Look up the words, and in the space provided write the dictionary respelling. Then pronounce each word to your instructor.

1. porphyry_____   6. syzygy_____

2. potpourri_____   7. paroxysm_____

3. palanquin_____   8. dishabille_____

4. ytterbium_____   9. sybarite_____

5. picot_____   10. piscine_____

Record the number of correct answers here and on page 207.

Exercise 31: _____out of 20 correct

Posttest A

Below you will find a list of words. Rewrite the words in syllables.

Example: particular *par/ti/cu/lar*

1. remarkable_____
2. rabbit_____
3. excavation_____
4. provision_____
5. preventive_____
6. palatial_____
7. disagreement_____
8. misleading_____
9. pitched_____
10. whistle_____
11. murmur_____
12. fabric_____
13. broken_____
14. doghouse_____
15. fireplace_____
16. needed_____
17. knuckle_____
18. uneven_____
19. transform_____
20. support_____
21. blushing_____
22. impolite_____
23. tormented_____
24. pardon_____
25. meter_____
26. trickle_____
27. housekeeper_____
28. misspell_____
29. misspelled_____
30. marvelous_____

Posttest B

Below is a list of nonsense words. Rewrite these words in syllables.

Example: prolip *pro/lip*

1. morlep_____
2. barkle_____
3. sunnip_____
4. sifol_____
5. drapost_____
6. stickle_____
7. cowhome_____
8. depicment_____
9. rehoptive_____
10. gothel_____

Posttest C

Look at the following dictionary respellings. If necessary, use the pronunciation key found in this chapter to help you pronounce the word. Read the words to your instructor.

1. (sĭn′ ə mə)
2. (ē kwəl)
3. (kəm pīl′)
4. (kə răl′)
5. (bā ə nĕt)

6. (rĕv′ ə lē)
7. (pûr′ sə kyo͞ot′)
8. (mĭl yə nâr′)
9. (fŏl′ ōd)
10. (ko͝osh′ ən)

Posttest D

Look up the following words in a dictionary. Write the dictionary respellings and pronounce the words to your instructor.

1. opulent_____

2. minutiae_____

3. herbaceous_____

4. croupier_____

5. chaos_____

6. celadon_____

7. phlebitis_____

8. pterodactyl_____

9. martial_____

10. miscellany_____

Compare your answers with those given on page 206. Place a checkmark by the number of your correct answer. Count the number correct and record that number here and on page 208.

Posttest A: _____out of 30 correct
Posttest B: _____out of 10 correct
Posttest C: _____out of 10 correct
Posttest D: _____out of 10 correct
Total: _____out of 60 correct

If you got 54 or more correct, you have successfully completed the last chapter of this worktext. Congratulations!
If you got less than 54 correct, talk with your instructor.
Show your instructor the summary sheet on page 208 on which you have recorded your scores for all the exercises and tests.

Answers to Exercises Not on the Skilltape

Exercise 3

1. flash/light	3. class/room	5. cow/boy	7. box/car	9. light/house
2. beef/steak	4. gold/fish	6. base/ball	8. eye/brow	10. ear/ring

Exercise 4

Possible answers: treetop, doorknob, lipstick, handstand, seafood, rainbow, eyesight, staircase, mousetrap, cowgirl
Check your dictionary to confirm any others you come up with.

Exercise 5

1. un(tie)	3. dis(play)	5. (man)hood	7. in(side)	9.(fool)ish
2. re(cover)	4.(kind)ness	6. de(part)	8.(nice)ly	10.(loud)er

Exercise 6

1. disagree	3. refill	5. greatest	7. unlock	9. display
2. graceful	4. swiftly	6. helpless	8. gardener	10. sweeten

Exercise 7

1. 2, ed	3. 2, d	5. 1, t	7. 2, ed	9. 1, t
2. 1, t	4. 2, ed	6. 2, d	8. 2, d	10. 3, ed

Exercise 8

1. 2	3. 1	5. 1	7. 1	9. 2
2. 1	4. 2	6. 2	8. 1	10. 1

Exercise 9

1. swim + ing	3. wrap + ing	5. drop + ing	7. snap + ed	9. scrap + ing
2. shop + ed	4. plan + er	6. run + er	8. fat + est	10. thin + est

Exercise 10

1. cold + est	3. stand + ing	5. greet + ing	7. loop + ed	9. herd + ed
2. great + er	4. dark + est	6. bead + ed	8. hard + er	10. sweet + est

Exercise 11

1. file + ing	3. skate + er	5. drive + ing	7. ride + ing	9. fine + est
2. waste + ed	4. taste + ed	6. brave + est	8. skate + ing	10. joke + er

Review Exercise 2

1. repress*ed*, 2
2. displeas*e*, 2
3. hom*e*less, 2
4. dera*il*, 2
5. unse*e*ming, 3
6. insid*e*, 2
7. misfir*e*, 2
8. rega*in*, 2
9. fa*i*rest, 2
10. tre*a*ted, 2

Review Exercise 3

	Prefix	Base Word	Suffix		Prefix	Base Word	Suffix
1.	re	fresh	ing	11.	dis	mount	ed
2.	mis	spell	ed	12.		fresh	ness
3.	mis	take	en	13.		fresh	est
4.	re	shape	ed	14.	dis	taste	ful
5.		pain	less	15.	for	got	en
6.	dis	miss	ed	16.		swift	er
7.	re	place	ed	17.	un	change	ing
8.	de	part	ed	18.	mis	print	ed
9.		tap	ing	19.		thank	less
10.	un	feel	ing	20.	re	train	ed

Exercise 12

1. bat/ter
2. can/non
3. pic/nic
4. sel/fish
5. sus/pect
6. lad/der
7. har/bor
8. cin/der
9. sup/per
10. gob/let

Review Exercise 4

1. sis/ter
2. door/knob
3. ham/mer
4. mean/ing
5. per/haps
6. can/cel (The first *c* has a *k* sound; the second *c* has an *s* sound because it is followed by *e*.)
7. en/ter
8. part/ed
9. shopped—one syllable
10. re/mark
11. fore/cast
12. de/part
13. dark/ness
14. pil/low
15. start/er
16. oat/meal
17. stoned—one syllable
18. pea/nut
19. wis/dom
20. mis/spelled

Exercise 15

1. crack/le
2. han/dle
3. scram/ble
4. pud/dle
5. trick/le
6. thim/ble
7. bi/ble
8. fa/ble
9. ti/tle
10. speck/le

Exercise 16

1. hun/dred
2. ze/bra
3. bush/el
4. mon/ster
5. por/tray
6. or/chard
7. con/tract
8. se/cret
9. oth/er
10. smoth/er

Review Exercise 5

1. gro/cer	5. eye/sight	9. riv/er	13. speck/le	17. mois/ture
2. pre/cook	6. hope/less	10. ro/tate	14. count/ed	18. hand/some
3. spot/ted	7. mas/ter	11. re/read	15. scram/ble	19. oat/meal
4. cheer/ful	8. stu/dent	12. pun/ish	16. neat/ness	20. un/fair

Exercise 17

1. i	3. e	5. e	7. i	9. i
2. e	4. i	6. e	8. i	10. e

Exercise 18

1. kind/ly, *e*	3. gra/vy, *e*	5. dai/ly, *e*	7. sup/ply, *i*	9. twen/ty, *e*
2. wit/ty, *e*	4. fly/ing, *i*	6. re/ply, *i*	8. late/ly, *e*	10. fif/ty, *e*

Exercise 19

1. tax	3. party	5. glass	7. brush	9. belt
2. rabbit	4. cross	6. candy	8. camel	10. penny

Exercise 20

1. bod/ies	3. cop/ies	5. speech/es	7. mar/ries	9. coach/es
2. inch/es	4. frogs	6. arm/ies	8. witch/es	10. girls

Exercise 21

1. stōv̸e	3. glăd	5. măn	7. spē̸ed	9. brŭnt
2. ĕnd	4. wīf̸e	6. lō̸af	8. shŏck	10. mūt̸e

Exercise 22

1. ē	3. ā	5. i	7. ī	9. o
2. ū	4. ō	6. e	8. u	10. a

Exercise 23

1. coma	2. cabin	3. medal	4. minus	5. robin

Exercise 24

1. ap'/ple	3. kit'/ten	5. a/way'	7. den'/tist	9. per/haps'
2. pic'/ture	4. ta'/ble	6. emp'/ty	8. win'/dow	10. po/lite'

Exercise 25

1. a/muse'	3. pa/rade'	5. cli'/mate	7. pitch'/er	9. bot'/tle
2. met'/al	4. stan'/za	6. co'/bra	8. bee'/tle	10. e/vade'

Exercise 26

1. su/per/man 3. black/ber/ry 5. bas/ket/ball 7. loud/speak/er 9. gen/tle/man
2. grand/moth/ 4. ev/er/green 6. can/dle/light 8. drill/mas/ter 10. mar/ket/
er   place

Exercise 27

1. truth/full/ness
2. use/ful/ness
3. watch/ful/ly
4. play/ful/ness
5. re/fill/a/ble
6. con/struc/tion
7. wash/a/ble
8. pre/heat/ed
9. un/fair/ly
10. un/like/ly
11. trans/port/a/
ble
12. ex/cite/ment
13. dis/a/gree/
ment
14. sub/hu/man
15. pro/duc/tion
16. pro/tec/tive
17. in/ter/ac/tion
18. pre/dic/tion
19. trans/fu/sion
20. re/spect/a/
ble

Exercise 28

1. ar/ti/fi/cial
2. sub/stan/tial
3. sen/si/tive
4. break/age
5. con/fi/den/tial
6. con/sti/tu/tion
7. dis/grace/ful
8. in/ex/pert/ly
9. dis/a/gree/a/
ble
10. bag/gage
11. in/ad/vis/a/
ble
12. in/dus/tri/ous
13. de/par/ture
14. con/clu/sion
15. trans/fer/a/
ble
16. nic/o/tine
17. ad/e/quate
18. de/li/cious
19. ath/let/ic
20. ex/ot/ic

Exercise 29
Part A

1. 3
2. 3
3. 3
4. 3
5. 3
6. 3
7. 2
8. 2
9. 2
10. 3

Part B

1. mag/a/zine
2. oc/u/list
3. wil/der/ness
4. af/ford/ed
5. trum/pet/ed
6. re/veal/ing
7. com/pound
8. knuck/le
9. e/quipped
10. ac/quaint/ed

Answers to Pretests and Posttests

Pretest A

1. 2	3. 2	5. 2	7. 2	9. 4
2. 2	4. 2	6. 3	8. 1	10. 1

Pretest B

1. buck/le	5. foot/ball	9. train	13. re/port/er	17. sim/ple
2. start/ed	6. au/to/mo/bile	10. lem/on	14. hu/man	18. cam/pus
3. ma/ple	7. spi/der	11. shame/ful	15. sup/port	19. harm/ful
4. thou/sand	8. mid/dle	12. parked	16. stressed	20. toiled

Pretest C

1. smoth'er	3. sup'per	5. prefer'	7. amaz'ing	9. strong'est
2. ath'lete	4. allow'	6. chuck'le	8. intend'	10. misplace'

Posttest A

1. re/mark/a/ble	7. dis/a/gree/ ment	13. bro/ken	19. trans/form	25. me/ter
2. rab/bit		14. dog/house	20. sup/port	26. trick/le
3. ex/ca/va/tion	8. mis/lead/ing	15. fire/place	21. blush/ing	27. house/keep/ er
4. pro/vi/sion	9. pitched	16. need/ed	22. im/po/lite	
5. pre/ven/tive	10. whis/tle	17. knuck/le	23. tor/men/ted	28. mis/spell
6. pa/la/tial	11. mur/mur	18. un/e/ven	24. par/don	29. mis/spelled
	12. fab/ric			30. mar/vel/ous

Posttest B

1. mor/lep	3. sun/nip	5. dra/post	7. cow/home	9. re/hop/tive
2. bar/kle	4. si/fol	6. stick/le	8. de/pic/ment	10. goth/el

Posttest C

1. cinema	3. compile	5. bayonet	7. persecute	9. followed
2. equal	4. corral	6. reveille	8. millionaire	10. cushion

Posttest D

1. äp' yə lənt	3. hər bā' shəs	5. kā'äs	7. fli bīt' is	9. mar' shəl
2. mi nōō' shie	4. krōō' pē ā	6. sel' ə dän	8. ter ə dak' t'l	10. mis' ə lā ne

Your dictionary may use different symbols in its respellings than those we have used in *Word Attack*. If so, spend some time examining the dictionary's key to respelling. Once you have familiarized yourself with a set of symbols, it can be of great use in learning to pronounce new words.

SUMMARY SHEET

Chapter 8

Record your scores for each test and exercise.

Instructor's Comments

	Number Correct
Pretest A	_____out of 10 correct
Pretest B	_____out of 20 correct
Pretest C	_____out of 10 correct
Exercise 1	_____out of 20 correct
Exercise 2	_____out of 23 correct
Exercise 3	_____out of 10 correct
Exercise 4	_____out of 10 correct
Exercise 5	_____out of 20 correct
Exercise 6	_____out of 10 correct
Exercise 7	_____out of 20 correct
Exercise 8	_____out of 10 correct
Exercise 9	_____out of 20 correct
Exercise 10	_____out of 20 correct
Exercise 11	_____out of 20 correct
Review Exercise 1	_____out of 44 correct
Review Exercise 2	_____out of 21 correct
Review Exercise 3	_____out of 54 correct
Exercise 12	_____out of 20 correct
Exercise 13	_____out of 10 correct
Review Exercise 4	_____out of 38 correct
Exercise 14	_____out of 20 correct
Exercise 15	_____out of 20 correct
Exercise 16	_____out of 20 correct
Review Exercise 5	_____out of 40 correct
Exercise 17	_____out of 10 correct
Exercise 18	_____out of 30 correct
Exercise 19	_____out of 10 correct
Exercise 20	_____out of 18 correct
Exercise 21	_____out of 15 correct
Exercise 22	_____out of 10 correct
Exercise 23	_____out of 5 correct
Exercise 24	_____out of 10 correct
Exercise 25	_____out of 20 correct
Exercise 26	_____out of 10 correct
Exercise 27	_____out of 20 correct
Exercise 28	_____out of 20 correct
Exercise 29	
Part A	_____out of 10 correct
Part B	_____out of 10 correct
Exercise 30	_____out of 10 correct
Exercise 31	_____out of 20 correct

Posttest A   _____out of 30 correct
Posttest B   _____out of 10 correct
Posttest C   _____out of 10 correct
Posttest D   _____out of 10 correct